SCHOOL MANAGEMENT BY WANDERING AROUND

LARRY FRASE
ROBERT HETZEL

SCHOOL MANAGEMENT BY WANDERING AROUND

TECHNOMIC
PUBLISHING CO., INC.
LANCASTER · BASEL

School Management by Wandering Around
a **TECHNOMIC**®publication

Published in the Western Hemisphere by
Technomic Publishing Company, Inc.
851 New Holland Avenue
Box 3535
Lancaster, Pennsylvania 17604 U.S.A.

Distributed in the Rest of the World by
Technomic Publishing AG

Printed in the United States of America
10 9 8 7 6 5 4 3 2

Main entry under title:
  School Management by Wandering Around

A Technomic Publishing Company book
Bibliography: p.
Includes Index, p. 201

Library of Congress Card No. 89-51778
ISBN No. 87762-640-5

Table of Contents

Introduction

MANAGEMENT By Wandering Around (MBWA) is the catalyst that brings teachers, aides, parents, and administrators together in the pursuit of excellent schools. MBWA is an active person-to-person process that relies on deeds, involvement, and participation to create better schools. The leader who embraces MBWA does not just talk about his philosophy, he lives it. The MBWA leader possesses an honest awareness of self and how he affects others. He creates and clarifies new visions. He encourages and empowers others to join in the quest to capture visions and transform them into reality. The MBWA leader is aware of the power, worth, and value of people. He actively pursues the school's mission *with* people because he knows that leaders who lock themselves in offices and force their visions on others through power-play memos are seldom successful. The power-play executive scares no one and no one pays attention, and, worse yet, no one follows.

Effective leaders have practiced MBWA throughout the ages. Alexander the Great, when it was clear that his Macedonians were mutinying against his plans with the Persians, went directly to his men and spoke to them. He didn't send a memo or a messenger. As H. G. Wells (1961, p. 292) describes it,

> . . . with some difficulty . . . he brought them to a penitent mood and induced them to take part in a common feast with the Persians.

People desire a sense of involvement, a sense of importance, a sense that what they do makes a difference. Smart leaders nurture this drive, and teachers, possibly more than any other group, possess this drive. When recently asked about what teachers want, Gerald Dreyfuss (see Schwartz, 1988), the man who organized and implemented the Dade County shared decision-making program where schools run themselves and principals practice MBWA, stated that ". . . sure, money is important, but what teachers really want is some ability to shape what goes on in the workplace." MBWA embodies this "count me in, we can do it as a team" spirit. The MBWA leader wanders throughout the school and community because he knows that is where education takes place. The MBWA principal is out listening for hints and clues to strengths, weaknesses, problems, and solutions. He doesn't retreat to the hallowed walls of his office to cast aspersions or point fingers of blame in the tradition of Marie Antoinette and King Louis XVI. They did and were beheaded. The penalties are different today, but the message is clear. In a CBS special, February 4, 1988, America's perennial presidential candidate Pat Paulsen offered pithy, straightforward, disarming advice to nay-sayers and skeptics when he said ". . . get off your butts, Americans, stop griping and complaining, find a better candidate. . . ." The MBWA principal is off his seat and on his feet looking and listening for better ways to do things—wandering with a purpose.

MBWA is not based on years of research or numerous scientific studies. It is based on common sense and hundreds of years of experience (Peters and Waterman, 1982). It is not new, nor is it difficult to understand. But more often than not, it has been forgotten or put aside in favor of ethereal and seemingly more impressive activities which can be completed only behind closed doors. As a client of Peters and Austin said, "MBWA is a blinding flash of the obvious" (Peters and Austin, 1984, p. 3). It clarifies the techniques that successful school leaders and leaders of all institutions, groups, and organizations have been doing for a long time. Recent research, although not directly assessing MBWA per se, has confirmed MBWA's assumptions. Effective schools' research demonstrates the strong and definite correlation between effective schools and <u>leaders who develop and articulate the school's mission and energize others to pursue it</u> (Rutherford, 1985; Crim, 1981) and spend at least 50% of their time in MBWA activities in classrooms and hallways (McCurdy, 1983). Andrews and Soder (1986) found that minority and low socio-economic status students attain higher achievement scores in schools where principals 1) provide resources to accomplish the school's mission; 2) provide instructional leadership; 3) articulate the school's vision and establish high student and teacher expectations; and 4) practice MBWA by maintaining visible presence in classrooms and interacting freely with staff and students. Valentine et al. (1981) demonstrated that perceived administrative effectiveness is strongly correlated with time spent working with teachers to solve program and instructional problems, and Blaze (1987) demonstrated that basic MBWA characteristics such as accessibility, visibility, willingness to delegate authority, and efficient time management are characteristics of effective schools.

MBWA capitalizes on these research results. The MBWA philosophy places people in "keystone" positions. Successful schools owe their success to people, not award-winning architectural designs. People make things happen. Plans, whether they are essential elements of instruction, zero-based budgeting, or situational leadership, are inanimate things made by people and have value only when people bring them to life.

Making poor schools good and good schools great is the mission of this book. Very little "new" material is presented. The contents are tried and true. What is different is the focus. The MBWA leader strives for excellence and is a lifelong learner. Self-awareness, trust, clarity of mission, belief in people, and commitment to the pursuit of excellence are the MBWA trademarks for schools and pervade the contents of this book. Implementation of the MBWA philosophy does not require expensive equipment, a semester class at the local university, or a high-powered conference. It requires awareness that things can be better and that people are the source of solutions and success. The MBWA leader is out and about with a purpose, interacting with others, listening and using information to make things better, exciting people, and empowering them with authority to achieve excellence. Nurturing human potential, making the best use of existing resources, leading by doing, removing roadblocks, and confirming your belief in people's desire and ability to do a good job are the keys to excellence.

This book offers specific strategies and techniques for using MBWA to attain excellence. The building blocks of school excellence, caring, openness, trust, and authority of expertise, are discussed in Chapter I, and practical, easy suggestions are provided. Chapter I closes with an instrument for assessing the perceived value of these building blocks in a school.

Some leadership theories and styles are compatible with MBWA and some are not. This is the subject of Chapter II. Similarities and dissimilarities between the MBWA assumptions stated above and the Great Man theory, Theories X and Y, the Managerial Grid, and conflict management styles are presented. This is not a dreary, in-depth examination of leadership theory. The chapter focuses on the practical characteristics of these theories, and tests are provided for assessing the reader's leadership and management style as it applies to MBWA. Determining the degree to which your current leadership style is compatible with the MBWA philosophy presented in this book and determining changes which must be made to ensure greater compatibility are the objectives of Chapter II.

Chapter III deals with visioning and the effective school leader. Suggestions for developing a vision and communicating it so that others follow are presented and discussed. Great leaders have a vision for their organizations; they translate it into everyday language, articulate it with clarity and passion, and energize others to make it a reality. Clear-cut steps for accomplishing this are presented in Chapter III.

The topic of promoting the improvement work ethic and the necessity of viewing learning as a lifelong process are addressed in Chapter IV. What motivates teachers? Why did they select teaching as their career? How do these motivations relate to professional development? What are the legitimate purposes of professional development programs? What are the hallmarks of high-quality professional development programs? How should content of training programs be determined? Answers to all of these are presented in Chapter IV.

MBWA is not to be confused with "aimless wandering"; instead, it involves a plan. Key focal points for MBWA in schools are presented in Chapter V.

Successful schools are a direct result of high-quality teachers doing their job well. Although we would like to think that all teachers are of "high quality," they are not. At the same time, the authors contend that administrators have no greater responsibility than placing competent teachers in the classroom. The sensitive subject of dealing with the marginal teacher is addressed in Chapter VI. Practical advice regarding how to recognize marginal teachers and strategies for dealing with them from the time of early detection through improvement or dismissal are presented.

The final chapter reviews specific techniques for making the best use of time and avoiding pitfalls that can trap and immobilize the school administrator. Strategies for freeing time for MBWA are presented. Strategies for effective planning of time in the office and in meetings are presented.

REFERENCES

ANDREWS, R. L., R. Soder and D. Jacoby. "Principal Roles, Other In-School Variables, and Academic Achievement by Ethnicity and SES." Paper presented at the Annual Meeting of the American Educational Research Association, San Francisco, April 1986.

BLAZE, J. J. "Dimensions of Effective School Leadership: The Teacher's Perspective," *American Educational Research Journal*, 24:4, 589–610 (1987).

CRIM, A. A. "A Community of Believers," *Deadalus*, 110:4, 145–162 (Fall 1981).

McCURDY, J. *The Role of the Principal in Effective Schools: Problems and Solutions*. Arlington:American Association of School Administrators (1983).

PETERS, T. and R. Waterman. *In Search of Excellence: Lessons from America's Best-Run Companies*. New York:Harper-Row (1982).

PETERS, T. and N. Austin. *A Passion for Excellence*. New York:Random House, p. 426 (1984).

RUTHERFORD, W. L. "School Principals as Effective Leaders," *Phi Delta Kappan*, 67:1, 31–34 (September 1985).

SCHWARTZ, A. E. "Editorial," *The Washington Post*. p. A21 (Jan. 29, 1988).

VALENTINE, J., D. C. Clark, N. C. Nickerson and J. W. Keefe. *The Middle School Principal*. Reston, VA:National Association of Secondary School Principals, p. 36 (1981).

WELLS, H. G. *The Outline of History*. Garden City, NY:Doubleday (1961).

CHAPTER
1

The MBWA Building Blocks of Excellence: Caring, Openness, Trust, and Authority of Expertise

VALUES are communicated with behavior, not words. Wandering around communicates what a principal believes, just as never leaving the office does. Effective schools, Cohen (1983) points out, are characterized by a distinct set of values: (1) a genuine caring about individuals, (2) a mutual trust, (3) an openness to differences in attitudes and feelings, and (4) a respect for the authority of expertise and competency. These values are the glue that holds a district, school, or classroom together and constitute the culture of the effective school. Preaching about them is not as important as living them from day to day. How, where, and with whom you spend your time tells more about your beliefs than oral pronouncements or written philosophies. Your values are seen in your deeds and actions.

CARING

In effective schools people care about people. Specifically, caring is a willingness to share or sacrifice time, money, energy, or other resources for the benefit of others. It is more than feeling empathetic; it's taking action on those feelings. Daily, principals have literally hundreds of encounters with students, parents, and employees, and each is an opportunity to strengthen or weaken this value. James Lewis (1985) cites five steps in establishing a caring relationship with employees: (1) attending, (2) listening, (3) responding, (4) personalizing, and (5) initiating.

Attending means being accessible and available. MBWA is intended to increase accessibility and go beyond the infamous "open door" policy and out into classrooms, lounges, and onto playgrounds. The second step, listening, is perhaps the most difficult. It requires principals to stop talking, to clear out mental clutter, and genuinely and non-judgmentally to show an interest in what is being said. After having heard what was said, a response is needed. This entails clarifying and probing, if necessary, and then sharing our reaction openly and honestly.

The fourth and fifth steps, personalizing and initiating, deal with ensuring that the interaction is focused on the individual's problem as opposed to generalizing and offering trite, irrelevant, or pat answers to serious questions or problems. Initiating means that the principal accepts responsibility to provide follow-up and to share in solutions and future contacts. The essence of Lewis' model is MBWA; taking time to be with teachers in their classrooms means you care. Contrary to its critics, it is not time-consuming; it's time invested in building strong relationships.

Below is a sampling of behaviors that enhance and impede the value of caring.

ENHANCERS

- starting a wellness program for employees
- having release time for committee work
- sending employees birthday cards
- using climate surveys
- visiting classrooms
- sending notes of appreciation and recognition

IMPEDIMENTS

- failing to keep people informed
- treating groups of employees differently
- gossiping
- holding people to excessively rigid requirements
- using daily schedules, i.e., 8:00 to 4:00
- failing to compliment a person for a job well done

TRUST AND OPENNESS

Trust is unquestionable dependability. When giving your word on an appointment, a promise of confidence, or a commitment to a level of performance, people can count on you. Trust also is communicated through your actions. As trust builds, so does the willingness to take risks. When teachers know they can count on the principal's support and interest, they become more willing to try new practices, to share information, and to extend themselves.

Openness to differing attitudes and feelings means that people recognize that there is no one best way and respect each other's right to be different. This results in a climate where innovation can take place and new ideas can thrive. The key to building openness is feedback: a willingness to give and receive relevant performance information.

The Johari Window below (Luft, 1970) is a useful model for describing the dynamics of building trust and openness through feedback and self-disclosure.

The window represents the sum total of all information known about a person, whether known by him or herself and/or others. Each pane in the window is described below.

The Public Self—This pane contains knowledge about yourself that you know and others know. This includes feelings and attitudes you've shared openly, as well as those implied by your behavior.

The Blind Self—This second pane reveals information other people have about you that you do not know. This knowledge is gained by inference and includes mannerisms and behavior of which you are unaware. This could include perceived favorites on the staff, being too strict or too lenient, or dealing with discipline, etc.

	KNOWN TO SELF	NOT KNOWN TO SELF
KNOWN TO OTHERS	THE PUBLIC SELF	THE BLIND SELF
NOT KNOWN TO OTHERS	THE PRIVATE SELF	THE UNKNOWN AREA

Used with permission: Luft, J. *Group Processes: An Introduction to Group Dynamics,* 3rd Edition. Mountain View, California:Manfield Publications (1984).

The Private Self—This pane includes information you have about yourself that others do not have because, intentionally or unintentionally, you've chosen not to share it. This could include attitudes about policies or people's performance or concerns and hopes you have for the school.

The Unknown Self—This last pane represents information about you that neither you nor anyone else knows. This includes your motivations, anxieties, unconscious needs, and ultimate potential. Although this pane can be reduced in scope and size, there will always be an area of the unknown (Luft, 1970).

Research at the Center for Leadership Studies has consistently shown a high positive correlation between openness of a leader's public self and that leader's effectiveness within that organization. The public self is expanded by diminishing the blind self through feedback and/or diminishing the private self through self-disclosure.

Feedback occurs when people perceive that a leader is receptive and they share information the leader does not know about himself. The critical elements are how receptive he is and whether action results as a result of hearing the feedback.

Of the myriad of feedback tools available none are more potentially helpful to a principal than distributing these simple open-ended questions:

My principal's greatest strength is . . .
My principal's greatest weakness is . . .
What I wish my principal would do more of is . . .
What I want my principal to continue to do is . . .
The biggest problem our school faces is . . .
The greatest strength of our school is . . .

Having the staff complete these anonymously can be enormously helpful and is also very courageous. Remember, don't ask if you don't want to hear. However, if you do ask, listen and then respond by correcting weaknesses and attacking problems. Feedback is essential to a healthy school and can be the springboard to professional and personal growth. It can also be temporarily hard on your self-image or ego but you can't get better if you don't know your weaknesses. Following is a model of the Johari Window under conditions of feedback:

THE PUBLIC SELF	THE BLIND SELF
THE PRIVATE SELF	THE UNKNOWN AREA

Self-disclosure occurs when a person trusts another to reveal aspects of himself the other person does not know. It is important the reader understands this means organizationally relevant information, not personal information. Self-disclosing your personal economic problems is not what is needed, but people need to know how the principal feels about the new curriculum adoption, whether he believes in corporal punishment, etc. The most revealing self-disclosure is how, where, and with whom the principal spends time during the school day. This is, again, the essence of MBWA. If children are important to you, you spend as much time with them as reasonable. If the new curriculum is important, you attend the in-services and observe curriculum implementation in classrooms. Not going into the classroom of the problem teacher communicates that poor teaching is tolerated or you don't know how to deal with it. How you spend your time self-discloses what you value. Below is the Johari Window under conditions of self-disclosure:

THE PUBLIC SELF	THE BLIND SELF
PRIVATE SELF	THE UNKNOWN SELF

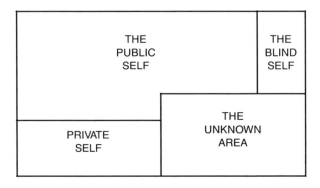

The effective principal uses MBWA both to build openness and to self-disclose. The Johari Window above represents the effective leader under conditions of self-disclosure and feedback. These are leader behaviors that build openness and trust. Time invested in pursuing them exhibits a caring and concerned attitude. Again, *doing* builds strong organizational cultures. MBWA is leadership in action, initiating and responding.

Finally, effective schools are characterized by a respect for the authority of expertise and competency. Teachers care less about personality than competency. Effective school leaders are perceived as instructional experts. Below are skills and/or behavior that define strong instructional leadership according to research carried out by the Northwest Regional Educational Laboratory (1984).

AUTHORITY OF STRONG INSTRUCTIONAL LEADERSHIP

- Instructional leaders portray learning as the most important reason for being in school; public speeches and writings emphasize the importance and value of high achievement.
- The leader has a clear understanding of the school's mission and is able to state it in direct, concrete terms. Instructional focus is established that unifies staff. The building leadership believes that all students can learn and that the school makes the difference between success and failure.
- Building leaders know and can apply teaching and learning

principles; they know research, legitimize it, and foster its use in problem solving. Effective teaching practices are modeled for staff as appropriate.

- Leaders set expectations for curriculum quality through the use of standards and guidelines. Alignment is checked and improved; priorities are established within the curriculum; curriculum implementation is monitored.
- Learning time is protected from disruption. Administrative matters are handled with time-conserving routines that don't disrupt instructional activities; time use priorities are established, widely communicated, and enforced.
- A safe, orderly school environment is established and maintained.
- Instructional leaders check student progress frequently, relying on explicit performance data. Results are made visible; progress standards are set and used as points of comparison; discrepancies are used to stimulate action.
- Leaders set up systems of incentives and rewards to encourage excellence in student and teacher performance; they act as figureheads in delivering awards and highlighting the importance of excellence.

Of the attributes listed above, none is more critical to building excellence than a knowledge of current research on teaching, learning, and leadership. Strong leaders exhibit a commitment to the improvement ethic: that competency is a lifelong journey.

ASSESSING THE BUILDING BLOCKS OF EXCELLENCE

On the following page is a sample instrument designed to access the perceived strength of caring, openness, trust, and respect for expertise in a school. Individuals rate the strengths placed on each value and identify specific practices that inhibit and/or enhance it.

A good technique is to have the staff complete the instrument individually and in small groups and share their ratings and the most significant enhancer and inhibitor for each value. The list presented earlier may be useful at this point. Next, the group should identify one suggestion to strengthen each value. These

SCHOOL CULTURE ASSESSMENT

Name (optional)_____

Position _____

Date_____

VALUE	ENHANCERS	INHIBITORS	SUGGESTIONS
My perception of these values in our school.	Conditions and practices that exist now that enhance or strengthen it.	Conditions and practices that exist now that inhibit or weaken it.	Ideas that I personally could try.
1. Caring Reaching out to one another, honest listening and responding. Weak Strong 1 2 3 4 5			
2. Openness to differences Acceptance of personal and professional differences. Weak Strong 1 2 3 4 5			
3. Trust Unquestionable dependability to be there, to support one another. Weak Strong 1 2 3 4 5			
4. Respect for the authority of expertise. Making decisions based on research and knowledge, as belief in continuous improvements. Weak Strong 1 2 3 4 5			

should be shared with the local staff, prioritized, and an action plan developed.

Effective schools are built on strong cultures, cultures that emphasize caring, trust, openness, and a respect for the authority of expertise. This foundation is built through effective leadership and MBWA can be a primary building tool. Leadership theories seem countless, and volumes have been written on the subject. Just as some leadership styles are better than others, some fit the MBWA philosophy and some do not. Leadership basics are addressed in the following chapter and you will have an opportunity to identify your style and ensure the proper "fit" for MBWA.

REFERENCES

BOSHEAR, W. C. and K. G. Albrecht. *Understanding People: Models and Concepts.* La Jolla:University Associates, pp. 85–89 (1988).

BREDESON, P. V. "Communications as a Measure of Leadership in Schools: A Portraiture of School Principals." *High School Journal.* 71:178–186 (April/May 1988).

COHEN, M. "Instructional Management and Social Conditions in Effective Schools." Paper prepared for the National Institute of Education, Washington, D.C. (1983).

DARESCH, J. C. "Collegial Support: A Lifeline for the Beginning Principal." *NASSP Bulletin.* 72:84–87 (November 1988).

LEWIS, J. *Excellent Organizations: How to Develop and Manage Them Using Theory Z.* New York:J. L. Wilkerson Publishing Company, pp. 21–37 (1985).

LUFT, J. *Group Process: An Introduction to Group Dynamic.* San Francisco:Mayfield Publishing Company (1984).

Northwest Regional Educational Laboratory. *Onward to Excellence: Making Schools More Effective.* Portland, Oregon (April, 1984).

CHAPTER
II

MBWA and Your Leadership Style: The Critical Fit

WHAT are the characteristics of a successful leader? On many occasions as speakers, the authors have asked members of the audience to list the four characteristics of a successful leader. To make the experience a bit more engaging, we announce that we are willing to take bets that no two lists will be the same or that no two characteristics will be present on each member's list. We have never lost the bet. What does this say about leadership? It says that it means a lot of different things to different people. For instance, compare the two lists below.

LIST A	LIST B
Dynamic	Has a vision
Considerate	Task oriented
Directive	Good people skills
Has vitality	Is democratic

It is doubtful that anyone would argue that these are not important characteristics of an effective leader. Ask any two "experts" on leadership to generate the list and the results will likely be equally as divergent.

Prior to 1960, studies of leadership traits were very common and considered the source of "truth" about what makes good leaders. Historians and biographers wrote about the great leaders long before the invention of the printing press. It was once thought that great leaders were "born," not trained, and were attracted to their role in life by a magical magnetism. This surrealistic notion was labeled the "Great Man" theory of leadership.

This theory emanated from the study of significant historical figures. What did leaders such as Caesar have in common with Alexander the Great? What did these two famous leaders have in common with Napoleon? The "Great Man" theory of leadership was based on the comparative approach. The common denominator for distinction was inherited capabilities which destined them to become great leaders. It was believed that the great leaders were endowed with unique capabilities that set them apart from the common masses. The "Great Man" theory led to the trait theory. What traits did the aforementioned greats—Caesar, Alexander the Great, and Napoleon—have in common, aside from their military feats? Let's examine common traits held by all three and see if they would be useful in screening for prospective superintendents or principals. Consider yourself; would you meet the criteria for a "great leader"?

(1) Each of these great leaders was left-handed. You lefties are still in the running.

(2) Each was relatively short, even for his time. If you are shorter than average, you are still in the running.

(3) All three contacted venereal disease. We hope you do not qualify under this criterion.

So much for the value of the "Great Man" theory of leadership.

In a more serious vein, the trait theory of leadership was based on the assumption that there were certain personality characteristics that could predict success in leadership positions. Leaders in all kinds of settings and organizations were studied, ranging from schools to military services and from banks to farm machinery companies. Every imaginable trait seems to have been considered, including height, weight, state of health, intelligence, self-confidence, sex, personality type, and many others. Burke (1980, p. 175) concluded that the leadership trait studies revealed very little, with the exception of a few observations such as:

(1) Taller people are more likely to be successful people, although they are also more likely to have an opportunity for leadership.

(2) Successful leaders are more outgoing than their followers in certain situations but not in others.

(3) Leaders tend to be more intelligent than the average person, but there is no positive correlation between success and I.Q.'s above 115.

The trait theory was slowly, and understandably, dismissed. In 1948, Ralph Stogdill concluded that there is little reason to believe that traits and the ability to lead are related. Richard Mann in 1959 and Bernard Bass in 1960 cast their vote for the same conclusion. Warren Bennis and Burt Nanus (1985, p. 4) recently echoed the conclusion in the following:

> Today we are a little closer to understanding how and who people lead, but it wasn't easy getting there. Decades of academic analysis have given us more than 350 definitions of leadership. Literally thousands of empirical investigations of leaders have been conducted in the last seventy-five years alone, but no clear and unequivocal understanding exists as to what distinguishes leaders from non-leaders.

Now, knowing that your height, weight, facial characteristics, confidence level, etc. alone cannot predict your success as a leader, consider just a few of the well-documented ideas from leadership and management studies to help you assess your leadership style and where you are in relation to these studies and, ultimately, in relation to MBWA.

ASSESSING YOUR LEADERSHIP STYLE

THEORY X AND THEORY Y: VIEWING PEOPLE AS PEOPLE, NOT AS CRETINS

The purpose of the remainder of this chapter is to assess your leadership style, the prerequisites to successful MBWA. Three activities are provided; each is designed to assess an important element of your leadership style and readiness for MBWA. Are you a Theory X or a Theory Y type? What is your balance between concern for production and concerns for people? And, what is your conflict management style?

In 1911, Frederick Taylor founded and popularized the notion of scientific management. This theory espoused the idea that the best way to increase output was to improve techniques or methods used by workers and was interpreted to mean that people were to be manipulated and used as instruments or machines by leaders. The key to scientific management was the metaphor "man as machine." In 1957, Douglas McGregor renamed this philosophy as Theory X and rejected it as an inhumane view of mankind. He proposed Theory Y which represents an opposite view of the nature of man as it relates to the workplace.

The first exercise for assessing your leadership style is to read the following characteristics and check those that describe you. Use your first impressions in selecting your answers.

Theory X and Y Characteristics

1. __The only interest of the organization is economy.
2. __People are not by nature passive or resistant to organizational needs.
3. __Work is natural for people if the conditions are favorable.
4. __Leaders must threaten and dominate employees to motivate them.
5. __The average man has the capacity to be creative.
6. __The average man is indolent by nature.
7. __The average man lacks ambition.
8. __The average man is self-centered and cares little about the organization.
9. __The average man is gullible and not very bright.
10. __Motivation occurs at the social, esteem, and self-actualization levels, in addition to the physiological and security levels.
11. __People can be self-directed and creative at work if properly motivated.

SCORING. The highest score possible is 5 and the lowest is –6. Give yourself one point for each of the following items that you checked: 2, 3, 5, 10, and 11. These items reflect the basic tenets of theory Y. Give yourself a –1 for each of the theory X items: 1, 4, 6, 7, 8, and 9. Figure the algebraic total for the two sets of items. Example: If the total for the theory Y set is +5 and the total for theory X is –1–the score is +4. Plus three is the minimum acceptable score. The higher your score, then the higher your Theory Y inclinations. Scores of less than +3 reflect Theory X tendencies.

Theory Y leaders are "people" types and are the people who should be out walking around interacting with others. Theory Y leaders believe in people, they believe people can be self-directed and creative, they believe people can enjoy work if the conditions are favorable, that people are not resistant to change or organizational needs, and that man is intrinsically motivated to achieve goals for himself and the organization. All Theory X beliefs have been considered "taboo" for many years in that they reflect a negative view of people. In fact, Theory X types should not practice MBWA. If you are a Theory X prototype, stay in your office and let someone else do the MBWA-ing. Wandering around threatening teachers, and treating them as if they were lazy ingrates will set your school back one hundred years and shatter any trust (see Chapter I) which may exist. This is, of course, tongue in cheek, but not totally. No leadership theory since the early 1900's has favored the Theory X style, and current leadership gurus such as Bennis and Nanus (1985), Peters (1987), Hersey and Blanchard (1982), and others call for Theory Y and rebuke Theory X. If you are a Theory X type, we suggest you make plans for moving to Theory Y. It can be done.

THE MANAGERIAL GRID: CONCERN FOR PEOPLE AND GETTING THE JOB DONE

Now that we are sure we are all certifiable Theory Y types, a basic MBWA characteristic, in that we believe in the worth, integrity, intelligence, and work ethic of people, let's examine the way in which this belief in people interacts with the leader's recognition that the organization has a mission and the leader's job is to lead people in the attainment of that mission. Concern for people is requisite to successful leadership, but concern for people only, the far left extrapolation of Theory Y, dooms the organization to failure. Under this form of leadership, the organization will fall short of accomplishing its mission—the school's long-term vision of what the organization is or is striving to become. To help balance these concerns let's look at another dimension of leadership—attainment of the organization's mission.

Robert Blake and Jane Moulton (1964) developed a grid for helping leaders analyze their concern for people and concern for the mission of the organization. In the case of schools, the mission is educating young people. Blake and Moulton called this "concern for production" (see Figure 2.1). "Concern for people" is represented on the vertical axis and "concern for production" is represented on the horizontal axis.

It is obvious that both concerns are very important to the health and mission of schools. As leaders, we work with people (concern for people) for the education of students (concern for production) and these concerns are not isolated from each other. Instead, these concerns must interact constantly within leaders. Figure 2.2 shows The Managerial Grid® with the five leadership patterns most often observed in organizations. The first digit describes the leader's concern for production while the second describes the concern for people. The 1,9 leader has a very low concern for production and a very high concern for people. Each of the five is described below.

1,1 (lower left of Grid) is that of the administrator who is "going through the motions." This leader is not really involved in the organization's affairs and contributes little to it, in that he has little concern for either people or production.

9,1 (lower right of Grid) depicts the extremely "task oriented" administrator with little concern for subordinates or other people and intense concern for "getting things done." This administrator knows what needs to be done and directs people to accomplish the goals. In this leader's organization, "efficiency in operations results from arranging conditions of work in such a way that human elements interfere to a minimum degree." You've seen this principal or superintendent: directive, hard-hitting memos are common; any talk in the school is business and never personal or for pleasure; teachers are given little autonomy; school is a place for work, not to take care of personal problems. Holiday celebrations are also directive. An illustrative holiday party announcement might read: "There will be a holiday party and *you will* enjoy yourselves—Cheers!"

5,5 (center of Grid) represents the principal who is moderately concerned with production and with people. Production is typically adequately high to avoid sanctions and morale is "OK" and nothing more. The principal is not "sweetness and light" as in the 1,9 style and is mediocre at best. Conventional expectations are met. Test scores are average, morale is average, community opinion is average, and the principal's expectations are average. Don't

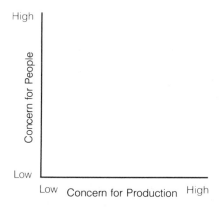

FIGURE 2.1. The Managerial Grid®.

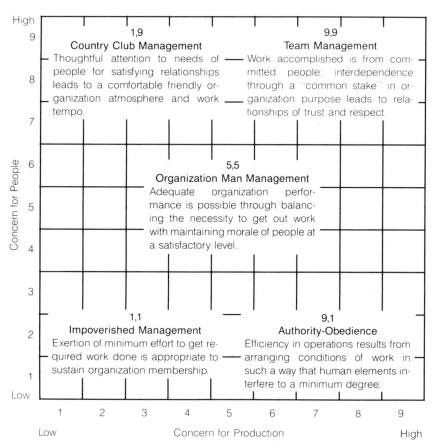

FIGURE 2.2. The Managerial Grid®. *Source:* Blake, R. R. and J. S. Mouton. *The Managerial Grid III: The Key to Leadership Excellence.* Houston:Gulf Publishing Company, Copyright © 1985, p. 12. Reproduced by permission.

rock the boat, we're not getting a whole lot accomplished, but I'm OK and you're OK.

1,9 (upper left of Grid) represents the "Country Club" atmosphere where the principal believes a happy teacher will get the job done and not cause him trouble. This principal is minimally concerned with the school, learning, and the community and devotes much attention to maintaining satisfying relationships with the staff by covering up for frequent late arrivals, unexplained absences, and rebuking parents' complaints that teachers are not well-prepared and frequently waste students' time with meaningless seat work. The payoff is that the teachers will say nothing when the principal takes off once or twice a week to play golf and tennis. This leader's goal is to maintain comfortable and friendly relationships in the hope that a comfortable organizational atmosphere and work tempo will result. This style is one of "you protect me, I'll protect you." The 1,9 administrator's MBWA style is more MBSG, Management by Smil'n and Grin'n. In this MBWA scenario, the administrator occupies his/her time extolling the virtues of the school, the teachers, the parents, and all others who touch the school and insuring that all people in the organization have a good time.

9,9 (upper right of grid) strongly reflects the Theory Y and MBWA orientation: teachers can be highly involved and enjoy their work, and the demands of production can coincide nicely with the needs that teachers have for satisfaction and recognition from their work. Work is accomplished by committed teachers. Interdependence occurs through a common belief in the school's mission and leads to relationships of trust and respect. The school fits the 9,9 style perfectly in that an abundance of research states that teachers are altruistic. They are intrinsically motivated to accomplish goals with their students—the mission of schools. The principal's job as a 9,9 leader is to help teachers accomplish their goal of helping students learn.

So what is your grid leadership style? To what extent do you emphasize concern for production and concern for people? Let's find out. The following items (see Whitefield, 1981) describe aspects of leadership behavior. Respond to each according to the way you would most likely act if you were the leader of a work group. Circle the response most common for you in each situation.

Key for Test

Always **(A)**
Frequently **(F)**
Occasionally **(O)**
Seldom **(S)**
Never **(N)**

1. Most likely act as a spokesman ....A F O S N
2. Allow staff complete freedom in work ....A F O S N
3. Encourage use of uniform procedures ....A F O S N
4. Permit staff to use judgement in solving problems .....A F O S N
5. Needle staff for great effort ....A F O S N
6. Let staff work as they think best ....A F O S N
7. Keep work moving at a rapid pace.................A F O S N
8. Turn staff loose on a job and let them go at it ....A F O S N
9. Settle conflicts when they occur ....A F O S N
10. Be reluctant to allow staff freedom of action ....A F O S N
11. Decide what to do and how to do it ....A F O S N
12. Push for increased production ....A F O S N
13. Assign staff to particular tasks ....A F O S N
14. Be willing to make changes ....A F O S N
15. Schedule the work to be done ....A F O S N
16. Refuse to explain my actions.....................A F O S N
17. Persuade others my ideas are to their advantage......A F O S N
18. Permit the staff to set its own pace ....A F O S N

Scoring your test

A. *Circle the item number for* 1, 3, 9, 10, 11, 15, 16, *and* 17.
B. *Write a 1 in front of the circled items to which you responded* S *or* N.
C. *Write a 1 in front of the items not circled to which you responded* A *or* F.
D. *Circle 1's which you have written in front of the following items:* 2, 4, 5, 6, 8, 10, 14, 16, *and* 18.
E. *Count the circled 1's. This is your score for concern for people.*
F. *Count the uncircled 1's. This is your score for concern for the production.*

Plot your score on the following grid. Place your concern for people on the horizontal axis and your concern for production on the vertical axis.

So how did you do? The average score for administrators is 3 on Concern for Production and 5 on Concern for People. If your

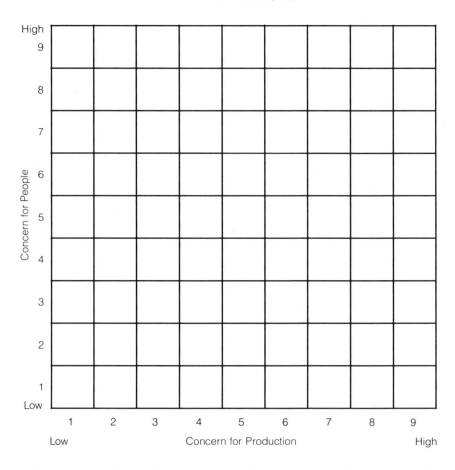

scores are not above the average or if they are out of balance, such as 4,9 or 8,3, we recommend that you spend more time analyzing your style and making the needed changes if you wish to become an effective school leader.

It is commonly accepted that high concern for both people and production is absolutely essential to successful school leadership and the MBWA philosophy. Blaze (1987), Andrews and Soder (1986), and Valentine et al. (1981) have demonstrated that principals' concern for production as demonstrated by accessibility, consistency, decisiveness, time management, and problem-solving orientation leads to increases in teachers' feelings of confidence and sense of professionalism while at the same time reducing feelings of tension, uncertainty, and anger. For the student, these characteristics lead to reduction of discipline problems, uncertainty, and wasted time while increasing time on task and acceptance of advice. Blaze (1987) has also shown that principals' concern for people as demonstrated by confrontation of conflict, recognition, participation, and willingness to delegate authority yields increases in teacher efficiency, professional self-esteem, and satisfaction while decreasing ambivalence, goal uncertainty, competition, defensive clique formation, and nonproductive conflict (back biting).

No creditable leadership theory denies the need for concern for production and concern for people, although the proponents of situational leadership (Hershey and Blanchard, 1982) and contingency theory (Fiedler, 1967) contend that one must be emphasized more than the other depending on the situation. The list of leadership theories seems endless: Theory Z, contingency theory, situational leadership, etc. Discussion of these is beyond the scope of this book. The point is that these two essential ingredients, concern for people and production, are equally important and form the foundation of the MBWA leadership philosophy.

MANAGING CONFLICT

The last characteristic requisite to successful leadership and MBWA is conflict management. Conflict situations are those in which the concerns of two people appear to be incompatible. The Thomas-Kilmann Conflict Mode Instrument (1975) is designed to

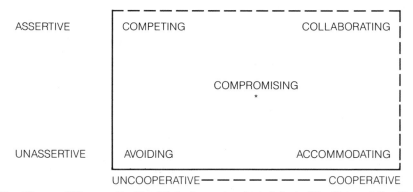

The Thomas-Kilmann Conflict Mode figure is adapted from "Conflict and Conflict Management" in *Handbook of Industrial & Organizational Psychology, Vol. II.* Marvin Dunnette, ed. Chicago:Rand McNally (1975).

assess administrators' preferred style of handling conflicts. There are two extreme behaviors a person may demonstrate in these situations: (1) assertiveness, where the person's goal is to satisfy his own concerns, and (2) cooperativeness, where one person attempts to satisfy the other person's concerns. These two dimensions are organized into the following two-dimensional model which identifies five conflict modes. Definitions of each mode follow.

Competing is assertive and uncooperative and is best illustrated when an individual pursues his own concerns at the other person's expense. Whatever power is needed is used to win, stand up for rights, defend a position, or simply try to win.

Accommodating is unassertive and cooperative and the opposite of competing. When accommodating, an individual sacrifices his concerns to satisfy those of another person. The accommodation mode is used when yielding to another point of view or simply being generous and charitable.

Avoiding is unassertive and uncooperative and means that the person does not address the conflict. Avoiding comes in the form of sidestepping or postponing a problem or simply withdrawing from a threatening situation.

Collaborating is both assertive and cooperative and involves an attempt to work with a person to arrive at a mutually fully satisfactory solution. Collaborating requires energy to look into the other side of the issue, to understand it, and gain insight as to why it is important to the other person so that an agreement can be reached. Resolving an issue in this manner can eliminate competition for resources or unhealthy confrontations.

Compromising is intermediate in assertiveness and cooperativeness and results in a solution which partially satisfies both parties. A person who compromises gives up more than when competing but less than when accommodating, addresses the issue more directly than avoiding, and doesn't explore it in as much depth as collaborating. Compromising may result in splitting the difference, exchanging concessions, or seeking a quick middle ground.

What is your style of conflict management? The following questions are designed to tell you just that. They represent thirty items comprised of two statements each. Select the response which you would be more likely to use, and circle the corresponding letter (A or B).

1. A. There are times when I let others take responsibility for solving the problem.
   B. Rather than negotiate the things on which we disagree, I try to stress those things upon which we both agree.
2. A. I try to find a compromise solution.
   B. I attempt to deal with the other person's and my concerns.
3. A. I am usually firm in pursuing my goals.
   B. I might try to soothe the other person's feelings and preserve our association.
4. A. I try to find a compromise solution.
   B. I sometimes sacrifice my own wishes for the wishes of the other person.
5. A. I consistently seek the other's help in working out a solution.
   B. I try to do what is necessary to avoid useless tensions.
6. A. I try to avoid creating unpleasantness for myself.
   B. I try to win my position.
7. A. I try to postpone the issue until I have had some time to think it over.
   B. I give up some points in exchange for others.
8. A. I am usually firm in pursuing my goals.
   B. I attempt to get all concerns and issues immediately out in the open.
9. A. I feel that differences are not always worth worrying about.
   B. I make some effort to get my way.
10. A. I am firm in pursuing my goals.
    B. I try to find a compromise solution.
11. A. I attempt to get all concerns and issues immediately out in the open.
    B. I might try to soothe another person's feelings and preserve our association.
12. A. I sometimes avoid taking positions which would create controversy.
    B. I will concede some of another's position if he/she lets me have some of mine.
13. A. I propose a middle ground.
    B. I press to get my points made.
14. A. I tell him my ideas and ask him for his.
    B. I try to show him the logic and benefits of my position.
15. A. I might try to soothe another's feelings and preserve our association.
    B. I try to do what is necessary to avoid tensions.
16. A. I try not to hurt the other's feelings.
    B. I try to convince the other person of the merits of my position.

17. **A.** I am usually firm in pursuing my goals.
   B. I try to do what is necessary to avoid useless tensions.
18. **A.** If it makes the other person happy, I might let him/her maintain his/her views.
   B. I will concede some of another's positions if he/she lets me preserve some of mine.
19. **A.** I attempt to get all concerns and issues immediately out in the open.
   B. I try to postpone the issue until I have had some time to think it over.
20. **A.** I attempt to immediately work through our differences.
   B. I try to find a fair combination of gains and losses for both of us.
21. **A.** In approaching negotiations, I try to be considerate of the other person's wishes.
   B. I always lean toward a direct discussion of the problem.
22. **A.** I try to find a position that is intermediate.
   B. I assert my wishes.
23. **A.** I am very often concerned with satisfying all our wishes.
   B. There are times when I let others take responsibility for solving the problem.
24. **A.** If the other's position seems very important to him, I would try to meet his wishes.
   B. I try to get him to settle for a compromise.
25. **A.** I try to show him the logic and benefits of my position.
   B. In approaching negotiations, I try to be considerate of the other person's wishes.
26. **A.** I propose a middle ground.
   B. I am nearly always concerned with satisfying all our wishes.
27. **A.** I sometimes avoid taking positions that would create controversy.
   B. If it makes the other person happy, I might let him maintain his views.
28. **A.** I am usually firm in pursuing my goals.
   B. I usually seek the other's help in working out a solution.
29. **A.** I propose a middle ground.
   B. I feel that differences are not always worth worrying about.
30. **A.** I try not to hurt the other's feelings.
   B. I always share the problem with the other person so that we can work it out.

SCORING

Circle the letters on the following table which you circled on each item of the questionnaire and total the number of items circled in each column in the spaces at the bottom of each column.

	COMPETING (FORCING)	COLLABORATING (PROBLEM SOLVING)	COMPROMISING (SHARING)	AVOIDING (WITHDRAWAL)	ACCOMMODATING (SMOOTHING)
1.				A	B
2.		B	A		
3.	A				B
4.			A		B
5.		A		B	
6.	B			A	
7.			B	A	
8.	A	B			
9.	B			A	
10.	A		B		
11.		A			B
12.			B	A	
13.	B		A		
14.	B	A			
15.				B	A
16.	B				A
17.	A			B	
18.			B		A
19.		A		B	
20.		A	B		
21.		B			A
22.	B		A		
23.		A		B	
24.			B		A
25.	A				B
26.		B	A		
27.				A	B
28.	A	B			
29.			A	B	
30.		B			A

Total number of items circled in each column:

Competing	Collaborating	Compromising	Avoiding	Accommodating
_____	_____	_____	_____	_____

The style which received the highest score is your most frequently used mode for managing conflict. Collaboration is the conflict management technique of the 9,9 management style. It is the mode highly successful administrators use in handling conflict and is recognized by conventional wisdom and management moguls. If collaborating was not your highest score, the authors suggest that you analyze your style and work toward more frequent use of collaboration.

Collaboration results in situations where both parties WIN. WIN-WIN situations are frequently desirable, although not always. Behavioral characteristics of WIN-WIN vs. WIN-LOSE groups and twenty-five steps for moving from WIN-LOSE to WIN-WIN are presented in Appendix A.

As desirable as collaboration is, it is not always the most appropriate style. Competing is appropriate when quick, decisive action is needed or when important issues such as cost cutting, firing, or disciplining an employee are unpopular. Compromising is appropriate when goals are moderately important and not worth the effort of trouble of the more assertive modes. Compromising is also appropriate when temporary solutions are needed and time-lines are tight. Avoiding, although the administrative wimp's way, is appropriate when an issue is trivial or when the issue simply cannot be won, and accommodating is appropriate when you are wrong and when building social credits and keeping harmony are more important than the issue.

SUMMARY

The effective leaders of today, yesterday, and tomorrow are those who make MBWA an integral part of the management style and mirror the basic tenets of Theory Y, the 9,9 leadership style, and the collaborating mode of conflict resolution.

Now that use of basic leadership qualities are assured, the role of the MBWA leader in creating and communicating a vision of what the organization should be, translating it into an operational mission and developing appropriate plans are addressed in the next chapter.

REFERENCES

ANDREWS, R. L., R. Soder and D. Jacoby. "Principal Roles, Other In-School Variables, and Academic Achievement by Ethnicity and SES." Paper presented at the Annual Meeting of the American Educational Research Association, San Francisco, April 1986.

BARTH, R. S. "Principals, Teachers, and School Leadership," Adapted from a chapter in *Building a Professional Culture in Schools*. A. Lieberman, ed., *Phi Delta Kappan*, 69:639–642 (May 1988).

BASS, B. M. *Leadership, Psychology and Organizational Behavior*. New York:Harper & Row Publishers, Inc. (1960).

BENNIS, W. and B. Nanus. *Leaders: The Strategies for Taking Charge*. New York:Harper & Row, 244 pp. (1985).

BLAKE, R. R. and J. S. Mouton. *The Managerial Grid*. Austin, TX:Scientific Methods, Inc. (1964).

BLUMBERG, A. *The Effective Principal: Perspectives on School Leadership*. 2nd edition. Massachusetts:Allyn & Bacon (1986).

BURDIN, J. L., ed. *School Leadership: A Contemporary Reader*. California:Sage Publications, Inc. (1989).

BURKE, W. "Developing and Selecting Leaders: What We Know," in *Behavioral Science and the Manager's Role*, William Eddy and Warner Burke. San Diego, California:University Associates, 375 pp., pp. 173–186 (1980).

CUBAN, L. *The Managerial Imperative and the Practice of Leadership in Schools*. Albany, NY:State University New York Press (1987).

FIELDER, F. E. *A Theory of Leadership Effectiveness*. New York:McGraw-Hill (1967).

FIELDS, G. M. "You Cannot Delegate Leadership," *Educ. Leadership*, 45:33–35 (March 1988).

GREENFIELD, W. ed. *Instructional Leadership: Concepts, Issues and Controversies*. New York:Allyn & Bacon (1988).

HARDEN, G. D. "The Principal as Leader/Practitioner," *Clearing House*, 62:87–88 (October 1988).

HERSEY, P. and K. Blanchard. *Management of Organizational Behaviors: Utilizing Human Resources*. Englewood Cliffs:Prentice-Hall (198?).

MANN R. D. "A Review of the Relationships between Personality and Performance in Small Groups," *Psychology Bulletin*, 56:241–270 (1959).

McGREGOR, D. M. *The Human Side of Enterprise*. New York:McGraw-Hill Book Company, pp. 37–57 (1960).

MURPHY, J. T. "The Unheroic Side of Leadership: Notes from the Swamp," *Educ. Urban Soc.* 20:276–93 (May 1988).

PASCARELLA, S. V. and F. C. Lunenburg. "A Field Test of Hersey and Blanchard's Situational Leadership Theory in a School Setting," *Coll. Stud. Jour.* 2:33–37 (Spring 1988).

PETERS, T. *Thriving on Chaos*. New York:Alfred Knopf (1987).

PITNER, N. J. "Leadership Substitutes: Their Factorial Validity in Educational Organizations," *Educ. Psychol. Meas.* 48:307–315 (Summer 1988).

RALLIS, S. "Room at the Top: Conditions for Effective School Leadership," *Phi Delta Kappan*, 69:643–647 (May 1988).

SHANKER, A. "Restructuring Leadership," *Coll. Board Rev.* 149:14–17+ (Fall 1988).

STOGDILL, R. M. "Personal Factors Associated with Leadership: A Survey of the Literature," *Journal of Psychology*, 25:35–71 (1948).

TAYLOR, F. W. *The Principles of Scientific Management.* New York:Harper & Row Publishers, Inc., pp. 42–43 (1911).

THOMAS, K. "Conflict and Conflict Management," in *Handbook of Industrial and Organizational Psychology, Vol. II.* Marvin Dunnette, ed. Chicago:Rand McNally (1975).

UBBEN, G. C. and L. W. Hughes. *The Principal: Creative Leadership for Effective Schools.* Massachusetts:Allyn & Bacon (1987).

VALENTINE, J., D. C. Clark, N. C. Nickerson and J. W. Keefe. *The Middle School Principal.* Reston, VA:National Association of Secondary School Principals, p. 36 (1981).

WEBSTER, W. E. *The High Performing Educational Manager.* Bloomington, IN: Phi Delta Kappa (1988).

WHITEFIELD, D. "Gutenberg Writing the 'Bible' on How to Select Management Teams That Mesh," *Los Angeles Times*, Part VI, pp. 3–5 (February 22, 1981).

CHAPTER III

MBWA with Purpose and Meaning

CREATING A VISION

GREAT leaders are visionary. They develop inspirational purposes for the organization based on study, creativity, and exposure to others' ideas. The vision is not always 100 percent theirs; in fact, they frequently borrow from others. They possess a unique ability to recognize great ideas and adapt them to the strengths and needs of their organization.

Visions for schools should not be confused with the typical general statements of educational philosophy, i.e., "the school is dedicated to the total personal development of each student" or "the school curriculum should be of adequate breadth to satisfy the intellectual and occupational goals for all youth who attend." These sentiments are nice, but neither adequately communicates direction or provides the philosophical criteria needed for decision making. The vision must focus everyone's attention on core values and purposes with which everyone can identify and from which everyone can gain direction for making decisions to help attain the vision.

Vision consists of mission (purposes), strategies, and core values. The mission is a deep abiding belief, a rallying point which touches deeply the hearts and souls of the people in the schools and the community. A school is only as good as the people in it and cannot improve until the people desire to do so. By stressing human and social values, the mission helps team members identify with a "cause" greater than themselves, to which they can become committed. The mission becomes a "calling," an inspiration to teachers, parents, staff, and students to make choices which lead to excellence. The good leader creates visions and excites others to follow.

Successful leaders of today's businesses and schools realize that no one organization can accomplish all or even more than a few visions. In fact, trying to do too much has led to failure for both businesses and schools. Peters and Waterman (1982) presented a powerful case for limiting the number of directions any one company should try to pursue. "Stick to your knitting" is the phrase they used to convey their message. The conglomerates of the 1960s which did not stick to their knitting, more often than not, ended in failure. Examples of over-diversification are endless. Liquor companies bought fast-food chicken franchises and tire companies bought destination resorts. The parent companies have now either sold their diverse acquisitions or have gone under. Rumelt's (1974) study of Fortune 500 companies resulted in the findings that moderate diversification may be healthy and that buying new companies for which the parent company has little expertise is destined for out-and-out failure or marginal success at best.

One of the most recent and illustrative examples of the stick to your knitting philosophy comes from Mita Copiers. Mita makes copiers, only. They wanted to communicate to the buying public that they specialize in one product with the implication being that they make better copiers than companies that offer more than one product. To do so, they used the tune and modified lyrics from a 1967 rock song by The Human Deinz entitled "Nobody But Me." The following is an excerpt from their version—"No No No":

—No! No! No! No! No! No! No! No! No!, We don't make TV's—like they do, we don't make cameras—like they do, we don't make microwaves—like they do, we don't make vacuum cleaners—like they do. We make copiers, just copiers, just copiers, just copiers—

The message is clear, they stick to their knitting. They make copiers only, and they do it well. The stick to your knitting philosophy applies to schools as proven by a brief look at the history of public education in America. Read on.

Community respect for the teaching profession took a hard, steep tumble in the 1960s as a result of the rebellious "touchy feely" era and an expanding curriculum based on students' and teachers' interests rather than students' needs. Relevancy was equated with fun and personal interests. The trend is reversing. Recent Gallup Polls (1986 and 1987) show that the public's esteem for teachers is on the upswing. The reason for the change in attitude is the return to what schools were originally designed and expected to do: teach the basics—reading, 'riting, and 'rithmetic. The first schools in our country were intended to teach these subjects and nothing else. The knitting was well-defined. Progressive educators influenced our schools greatly during the early and mid-twentieth century. The basics were neglected in favor of "natural unfoldment" as espoused by Rousseau. This lasted while expectations for the schools were expanded to include food service, medical care, pre- and after-school care, student and family counseling, bus service, career education, vocational education, fine arts, athletics, agriculture, leisure studies, family activities, bachelor studies, Baja whale watching, etc. (see Ornstein, 1985, for a discussion of the evolution of aims in education). The list is endless and resulted in nose dives for test scores during the 1960s and 1970s, resulting in a drastic loss of public respect for schools. The result is not unpredictable. Educators are trained to teach specific subject areas, not run buses, restaurants, or medical service operations and the like. Education became a giant conglomerate, and the effects were disastrous. Likewise, perfecting teaching is next to impossible if the subject is constantly changing or time for teaching is being usurped for other matters.

The academic spirit revisited education in the early 1980s. *A Nation at Risk* (1983) and the many other commission reports like it called for a return to the basics with a tightening of expectations and standards, similar to that called for by our founding fathers. There has been a return, although far from total, to the basics. This trend is spurred on by the finding that one of the key characteristics of effective schools is an "emphasis on the basics" (Robinson, 1985, p. 20). Former Secretary of Education Bennett's (1988) proposed curriculum for the mythical James Madison High School and the nation's high schools is likely to give the trend momentum: two years of foreign language, three years of mathematics, four years of English, four years of history, three years of science, two years of physical education, and one year of fine arts. Test scores have been on the rise since the early 1980s and the public respect for schools is also on the rise. The public favors the basics and doesn't have difficulty defining them (Gallup, 1987). The public wants schools to stick to the knitting.

Continuation of this focus will further elevate public opinion of America's schools. The concept of a focus, or vision if you will, is key. The school's vision is the glue which holds the organization together and produces consistent excellence. Any organization can accomplish one vision but not all visions. Education's shoulders are of a finite breath. Education can deliver the basics and a few select other expectations, but that's all. As Philip Altbach (1986) stated, we must say no to the endless requests to do more.

Those who want the schools to accept responsibility for a myriad of other chores won't like this response and will predictably assert that a focus on the basics is too narrow. Possibly the shortest and most effective response to this charge came from Ronald Edmonds (Brandt, 1982):

> . . . you have to earn the right to experiment with something as special as education. The way you earn it is just by teaching the kids to read and write.

Altbach (1986) echoes Edmonds' sentiments in the following response to requests for schools to accept additional burdens. "First of all, it must be recognized that schools can do one job best – that of educating children. The rest is extra."

The sophisticated guiding adages for further enhancing the public schools' esteem in the eyes of the public are: DEFINE YOUR VISION! DON'T BITE OFF MORE THAN YOU CAN CHEW! DO A FEW THINGS AND DO THEM WELL! DON'T OVERLOAD! DO WHAT YOU DO WELL!

The following from the Southern Bay School District in San Diego is a good example of a stick to your knitting mission statement:

> The South Bay Union School District provides for the educational needs of all students in the areas of basic skills and decision making; and encourages a desire for learning, positive social interaction and mutual respect. This mission is essential if our students are to become productive members of society with its ever changing technology.

In this statement, Superintendent Phil Grignon communicates a well-defined focus and a stick to your knitting attitude. The statement focuses the district on the basics. Student population in South Bay is 61% minority. Test scores have jumped to the 78th percentile in just three years, and the community attitude toward the district is vastly improved. The superintendent had a vision, he communicated it, and others followed. The students won.

The Catalina Foothills School District statement of philosophy listed the "basics" as its number one emphasis. Since doing so the percentage of students scoring in stanines 7–9 have tripled in mathematics, English, and reading. The board and superintendent set the vision, communicated it, and others followed. Again, the students won.

The support for having a well-defined mission statement derived from a vision extends far beyond philosophical bias and common sense to highly respected research. A well-articulated and actively communicated mission statement is possibly the most widely documented characteristic of effective schools (Brookover and Lezotte, 1979; Edmonds, 1979; Bossert, 1982; Lipsitz, 1984; Rutherford, 1985; Andrews and Soder, 1986). Rutherford (1985) in particular found that principals of effective schools gave definite and quick answers when asked to state the vision of their school: raising test scores, helping teachers adjust to a changing population, etc. Principals of less effective schools tended to pause and respond with a vague statement such as, "We have a great school and my job is to keep it that way." Instead of communicating vision and enthusiasm, the latter statement communicates mediocrity and lethargy. The former communicates energy and gives definite purpose and direction for what to look for while on MBWA outings. In contrast, the latter is fuzzy and says little about the school's purpose or successes and gives little direction for MBWA.

DEFINING AND OPERATIONALIZING THE VISION: THE PLANNING PROCESS

Purposes and strategies must be based upon core values in the school. Core values along with the purpose and strategies promote consistency among all members of the team: teachers, custodians, aides, volunteers, etc. Core values represent how people (parents, students, and non-parents) in the school and community should be treated. IBM's core value is "respect for the individual" and Hewlett-Packard's is "consider the need of the person at the next desk." These communicate the way people must be treated in order for the total group, the organization, to accomplish its mission. An administrator cannot communicate this by memo. The principal can communicate it through MBWA. The principal must be out in the classrooms, in the hallways, on the playgrounds, and in the community living and demonstrating it.

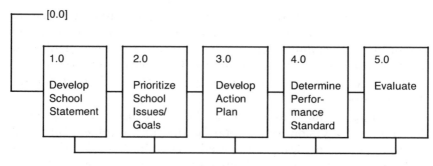

FIGURE 3.1

Read on; the next few pages deliver the "how to's."

Many processes are available for developing the mission and the strategies for attaining it. The process presented here is commonly known as strategic planning via the system analysis technique (see Figure 3.1). The advantages of strategic planning follow.

(1) Assesses school resources and allocates them on the basis of *how* to use them, *when* to use them, and in *what* amounts to attain the goals and the vision

(2) Allows administrators to define the interest groups and publics they wish to work with and for how long

(3) Focuses on results and is easily communicated to the constituency

(4) Helps separate the wheat from the chaff so that the job does not appear overpowering

(5) Gives school people and community members an opportunity to participate in decision making

(6) Opens the communication process within the school and community

(7) Permits making today's decision with the future in mind

(8) Pulls the school organization and community together so that it performs as a team

The advantages of strategic planning are many, but not magical. As with any other management process, it can be just another elixir. It requires hard work and tenacity, and it yields a valuable product.

The five major steps in this process are presented below in a system analysis mission profile (see Figure 3.1). A narrative explanation of each step follows.

DEFINING THE VISION: A MISSION PROFILE

STEP 1.0 – DEVELOPING THE MISSION STATEMENT

The desired product of step 1.0 is a mission statement which states the following in terms of what is desired for and from the school: the district's mission/philosophy, the differences between the school and private schools and other public schools, unique and common goals of the school, and the unique character of the community (Kaufman, 1988). The mission statement must be specific. It may be helpful to preface it with a philosophical statement, but the mission statement should be clear, devoid of jargon, and easily understood. Last, as previously stated, the mission statement must communicate the vision and serve as the rallying point for everyone's efforts.

The administrator's first step in developing a mission statement is to develop his own. This requires soul searching, deep thought, and exposure to ideas. Answers to questions such as the following will help. What is my vision for my school? What should the school look like? What should it do? What message and attitude should the school convey? How do I view the clients, the students, and the teachers? The core values must reflect the administrator's values and the administrator must be willing and excited to "live" them, to sell them.

It is likely that the district office has already accomplished some work which will give direction for determining the content of a mission statement. For example, has the district published a philosophy statement? Does a statement of district purposes appear in the board's policy notebook? If so, use this information to guide development of your mission statement. When the draft is complete, it is time to "test" it out. This is accomplished in two stages. First, bounce it off trusted colleagues. Select a few teachers, other administrators, and parents with whom you have an open relationship and great amount of trust and respect for their creativity and intelligence. The primary advantage of this approach is the privacy and confidentiality it affords. In the comfort of this setting, the administrator can voice far-out ideas and ill-formed thoughts without embarrassment or concern about stifling creative thought. Second, run it up the flagpole to see who salutes. This is an expansion of the first step and requires MBWA. After revision based on step one, take it a bit more public. Visit the teachers' lounge, the P.T.A. meeting, student council, etc. These are excellent opportunities to gather opinions. Start with lead-ins like "I've been thinking about . . ." or "I'd really like your reaction to . . ." thus leaving open the door to the broadest possible response and communicating that "This is my program, but it is not set in concrete. I value your thoughts."

The authors suggest that the mission statement must be a product of many people representing the various publics and interest groups in your community, including: parents; retired people; business leaders; community organizations such as the Junior League of Women, Rotary, etc.; and special interest groups, both agitators and friendly types (Wayson, Achilles, Pinnell, Lintz, Carol, and Cunningham, 1988, p. 28). See Appendix A for a review of the twenty-five steps to attaining win-win situations and the behavioral characteristics of win-lose vs. win-win groups. We strongly suggest that the committee members be community stakeholders and opinion leaders. Don't lock a group out because they have not been friendly or particularly supportive in the past. Locking them out may fuel their fire. Bringing them in will give you a chance to show off your school and gain their involvement and support. We caution against being standoffish. Listen closely to what they are saying. The fact that they disagree with you does not necessarily mean they are philosophically deranged or wrong. They may be able to help improve your school.

This is MBWA in action. As a leader, you will act just as Alexander the Great did when he sensed mutiny among his army. He went directly to his men and spoke with them, brought them to a penitent mood and induced them to take part in a common feast with the Persians. Being out and about with his men won a victory for Alexander. Practicing MBWA in the community may win a victory for your school.

If opening the doors to those you do not trust causes you severe discomfort, please review your scores on the conflict mode instrument in Chapter II. When you are right and well-prepared, the supposed enemy cannot harm you. Try Alexander the Great's strategy. Positive community relations is a basic characteristic of an effective school. The best place to start is teaming up with the community to determine the school's priority goals. Agreement on these and the action steps to achieve them will help develop that win-win relationship. Go to them and invite them in. Your openness may disarm them, and many hard feelings and misunderstandings will be overcome.

The first meeting of this group should include a description of the five steps of the project, their role in the project, an agenda for the meeting, and presentation of your mission statement—your vision. Other materials relative to the task (district policy statement of purposes, district mission statement, the school's previous mission statement, etc.) should also be available. See Chapter VII for strategies on fine-tuning your meeting plans.

Although you will have prepared a mission statement you are proud of, be open to criticism and changes, just as you were when you confided in colleagues and ran an early version of it up the flagpole. Depending on the quality of the committee members, changes will be suggested. Be open and process the information to arrive at a final document. Although you are the principal and responsible for the school, the final mission statement isn't going to be yours only; it belongs to the school, staff, and its patrons, in addition to you. Remember, you don't own the school; you were hired to lead it.

Developing a mission statement is generally iterative and will require you to call a couple of these meetings to review drafts which will improve with each review. Committee members will have ownership and be the school's most zealous sales force. The idea of sales is very important at this stage in some communities. Now is the time for the first press release announcing that a first-class school improvement process is being planned. Give the release to TV, newspapers, radio stations, and district newsletter staff. Give special attention to the local P.T.A. The media allows expansion of our MBWA capabilities, but the personal touch is needed in the local community. This is an important project; it is going to make the school even more effective and solve problems via a true grassroots team approach. Put your best foot forward. Let people know what you are doing. Doing so expands your MBWA coverage. Remember, you can't be everywhere. Let the media help. See Chapter VII for hints in developing press releases.

STEP 2.0 – PRIORITIZING ISSUES AND GOALS

This step demands that the mission statement be specific to allow comparison of the school's *status quo* with *what is desired for the school.* Once prioritized, the discrepancies between the status quo and what is desired become the goals or the issues the school will address. The same committee which composed the mission statement can conduct the initial comparison, but we suggest that the mission statement be taken to other community groups to insure that community concerns are reflected in the product of this step. An alternative is to develop a survey based on the contents of the mission statement and other aspects of the school. A section of a larger instrument designed to assess "communication" between the parents and the school is provided below. Parents are asked to respond to each statement twice, once to evaluate the school in regard to the statement and once to indicate its importance. Two complete surveys for elementary and junior high schools are presented in Appendices B and C. A sample of the survey format follows:

Several areas of interest have been identified in the questionnaire below. We would like to have an indication of your feelings about these areas and the importance you attach to them. In the center of the page is a series of statements. Please indicate your agreement or disagreement that each statement is true of Manzanita School *now* by marking the scale to the left. On the right of each statement, please indicate the importance you attach to it. Each statement should have two responses. Space has been provided for your comments and suggestions below each section.

Please circle the grade(s) that your child/children attend. K 1 2 3 4 5 6

A Strongly Agree	1 Very Important
B Agree	2 Important
C Disagree	3 Somewhat Important
D Strongly Disagree	4 Not Important
E Lack Info to Respond	

DO I AGREE OR DISAGREE　　　　　　　　　　HOW IMPORTANT IS
WITH THIS STATEMENT?　　　　　　　　　　　　AREA TO ME?

A　B　C　D　E　1. The school communicates clearly　　1　2　3　4
　　　　　　　　　its rules and standards of behavior
　　　　　　　　　to parents.

A　B　C　D　E　2. The school keeps parents informed　1　2　3　4
　　　　　　　　　of school activities.

A B C D E   3. Students have the opportunity to   1 2 3 4
                   communicate their interests and
                   concerns to teachers.

A B C D E   4. Students are kept informed of   1 2 3 4
                   their progress by teachers.

Comments: _____

           _____

           _____

Step 2.0 requires much administrative preparation. In addition to information derived from the survey, the committee is going to want to know how the school's test scores stack up with the national average and other schools in the district. A few graphs will help depict this very clearly. Other comparisons likely to be requested deal with discipline, special teacher F.T.E., class size, material allocation, curriculum and instructional resources, teacher quality, physical facilities, etc. Get these ready before the meeting; the committee will give you other ideas to keep you busy preparing for the next meeting. Another means of gaining very valuable data is a parent survey.

It is not uncommon for a subgroup to be generally petulant about the school and toss out general gripes and complaints. One ground rule should be that general gripes or complaints are not helpful in completing the process and cannot be accepted. Ask the members to be as specific as they can be. Statements must be specific to warrant inclusion in the action plan. See Chapter VII for use of ground rules when conducting meetings.

Having a facilitator may be desirable at this stage. Assess the attitude of the group and the prevailing politics. If it looks like the discussion could be heated or somewhat unruly, bring in a group facilitator. "Heat" does not mean that the meeting will be bad or should be cancelled. On the contrary, if heat does exist, it must be dissipated. Don't try to confine it and, for sure, don't fan it. A skilled group facilitator is needed in this situation to keep the focus off you. You are not the focus, the school is.

After the list of issues/goals has been hashed and rehashed, it is time to get on with setting priorities. Why set priorities? Why not tackle all those issues and accomplish all those goals? Because neither you nor the staff can do it all, that's why. Highly successful organizations keep their mission and visions simple and avoid a multitude of ramifications. Too many goals, too many directions, and too many details create confusion and overload management and staff. A good illustration is provided in the children's book and movie *Watership Down* (about a world of rabbits) where the characters can keep track of only seven things at once. After seven, they only count a "herarah," because any number larger than seven becomes indistinguishable. Thus, whether it's 8 or 800 or 8,000 doesn't matter—it's just a "herarah." For the rabbits in this book, there's a strong need to keep it simple (fewer than seven items). Humans have the same need. Administrators are constantly bombarded by a "herarah" of data, problems, and projects. Keeping it simple is not just important; it's the only way to survive *and* the only way for the school to achieve its vision. The committee may push for charging forth on all fronts, and it's the administrator's job to help them understand that time and resources do not permit doing an adequate job, let alone an excellent one, on an excessive number of goals. Selection of a few to tackle now, and development of a timeline showing when the others will be addressed will help the committee feel more comfortable with the idea of prioritizing.

At least three very effective prioritization processes exist to select from: forced pairing, Delphi, and the Phi Delta Kappa technique. Each employs group discussion and is designed to deliver group consensus.

Forced Pairing

This process is ideal for use by a committee of fifteen or fewer working on ten or fewer goals. The first step is to construct a matrix such as the one in Figure 3.2. Assign each goal a letter and list the letters along the horizontal and vertical axes in alphabetical order. Rank each issue on the vertical axis in comparison to each on the horizontal axis. For instance, the group will compare the importance of goal A with goal B, C, D, etc. If A is determined to be more important than B, write A in the common cell for goal row A as shown on page 41. After this is completed for each vertical cell, count the number of A's in goal row A, the number of B's in goal row B, etc. If the letter for goal A appears in more than 50 percent of the cells, it is selected as a high priority goal. Determining the priority ranking for the goals selected at this point is accomplished by ordering the goals by the number of times the letters appeared. Ties can be broken by a vote of the committee.

FORCED PAIRING

	A	B	C	D	E	F	G	H	I	J
GOAL A			C		E	F	G		I	
GOAL B	A				E	F				
GOAL C		B			E			H		J
GOAL D	A	B	C		E	F	G		I	J
GOAL E										
GOAL F			C		E		G	H	I	J
GOAL G		B	C		E			H	I	J
GOAL H	A	B		D	E			H		J
GOAL I		B	C		E				I	J
GOAL J	A	B			E					
TOTAL	4	6	5	1	9	3	3	4	4	6

FIGURE 3.2

A Delphi Process

In contrast to the forced pairing technique, the Delphi technique accommodates a larger number of goals and participants, encourages divergent and convergent thinking by directly involving participants in determining the goals from the beginning, and prevents domination of the process by ax grinders and other verbose nay-sayers and know-it-alls. In addition it serves as a vehicle for grouping the goals by topic, subject, or some other commonality. This is particularly useful if the committee has generated such a large number of goals that other ranking techniques cannot be used. For example, no valid group consensus technique exists for ranking large numbers of items, so the first step is to reduce the number of goals. The Delphi procedure accomplishes this by grouping the goals by theme and then ranking the groups. This process takes considerable time and organization but yields a valid product your community will appreciate.

Step 1. The large group is divided into 4, 8, or 16 sub-groups. The number of groups utilized depends on the number of total participants.
    a. Sub-groups should have about 5 members.
    b. The index cards are divided evenly among the sub-groups.

Step 2. Each sub-group is asked to examine each of the cards and arrange them into categories.
    a. Sub-group members decide categories.
    b. Sub-group members may determine the number of categories they desire.

Step 3. When each sub-group has categorized its cards, it combines with another sub-group.
    a. Categories are redefined and combined until the two groups reach consensus.
    b. This process is repeated until the entire group is reconstituted (8 groups combine to become 4 groups; 4 groups combine to become 2 groups; 2 groups become 1 group).

Step 4. When the group has reached consensus on the categories, they are listed on a chalkboard or overhead projector. The large group is again divided into sub-groups of 4, 8, or 16.

Step 5. Each small group is asked to rank order the categories by:
    a. Categories are rated on a scale of 1 to 5 (5 = the highest rating).
    b. Each group is limited to the number of points that can be assigned (this eliminates the tendency to assign 5 points to each item).
    c. Total points are determined by multiplying the number of items by $2\frac{1}{2}$ (10 items = 25 points).

Step 6. When each sub-group has rated the categories, the groups are combined, utilizing the same procedure as described in Step 3.

Step 7. When the large group finally gets together again, the categories rated by the sub-groups are combined into a group consensus rating.

The complete Delphi process starts with a step wherein the group participants write the goals. This substitutes for step 1.0 of the mission statement presented on page 34 and is described below.

Step 1. After the task has been explained, 3 x 5 index cards have been distributed, the number of goals to be written by each member has been determined and communicated, allow 20–40 minutes for the participants to write goals on the cards. Collect the cards and proceed with step 1 as stated previously.

The Phi Delta Kappa Goals and Objectives Model

The Phi Delta Kappa (PDK) Model differs from the Delphi technique in that it represents to the group eighteen very general and predetermined educational goals. At an introductory session the goals are discussed with participants, and an opportunity is given to add additional goals. Each participant is then given a set of eighteen goals, a value rater board, and forty-five points. The goals are ranked on a 1–5 point scale by each individual (point limitation = 45 points). Participants are next assigned to groups of four where the same process is repeated. The scores from each of the groups are computed and these totals provide the basis for the priority ranking.

Phase 2 provides for the rating of the eighteen goals. Participants are asked to respond to each of the goals as follows.

"In my opinion, how well are current programs meeting these goals?" Their responses are made on a scale of 1–15 that includes the following categories:

Extremely Poor	1–3
Poor	4–6
Fair, but more needs to be done	7–9
Leave as is	10–12
Too much is being done	13–15

Each goal rating is totaled and the mean is computed. Those goals receiving the lowest ratings are the areas of the greatest need.

The PDK Model is relatively easy to use; provides quantitative feedback on priorities; eliminates preparation of material, since complete packages are available for purchase; provides a packaged process for step 3 of the five-step process model presented in Figure 3.1; and by-passes the time-consuming stage of identifying goals. Plenty of goals have been developed by many districts and schools. Starting from the beginning need occur only when unique circumstances are present. Using predetermined goals can also be a weakness. School communities need ownership of their school's goals. The PDK process accommodates this need by permitting the addition and deletion of goals. Directions for dealing with the statistical differences resulting from the change in number of goals to be addressed are provided.

After the goals are prioritized, it's time to work on the action plan, which is outlined on the next page.

Facilities Improvement Management Legend

	Activity	Person Responsible	Due Date
10	Determine facility improvement projects	Principal	09-30-87
20	Determine projects to be completed by staff	Principal/Maintenance personnel	10-15-87
30	Determine projects to be completed by contractors	Principal/Maintenance personnel	10-15-87
40	Secure cost est. for 20 & 30	Lead maintenance person	11-15-87
50	Compare costs to available funds	Principal	11-25-87
60	Determine funds needed	Committee Chairperson	11-30-87
70	Determine fund raising strategies	Committee Chairperson	01-15-88
80	Organize fund raising teams	Committee Chairperson	01-30-87
90	Schedule improvement projects	Principal	01-30-87
100	Complete 70 & 80	as assigned	12-88

FIGURE 3.3 Action plan for facilities improvement.

STEP 3.0 – DEVELOPING A PLAN OF ACTION

The action plan is your road map for achieving the goals. The plan should state the sequence of steps to be followed for each goal, who is responsible for accomplishing each step, and the completion date for each step. The authors strongly suggest mapping the course of action in system charts or PERT charts with a management legend such as the one presented in Figure 3.3.

The advantages of developing a management plan are: (1) forces consideration of what is required to achieve the goal from beginning to end, (2) serves as a clear step-by-step master plan for achieving the goal, (3) is easily used for monitoring progress and adjusting the plan, and (4) is easily communicated to others so that their responsibilities and due dates are clearly defined. The person identified as the "person responsible" should not be expected to do all the work. Instead, this person is responsible for seeing to it that the activity is accomplished. Nearly all activities require team efforts of two or more people.

STEP 4.0 – DETERMINING PERFORMANCE STANDARDS AND EVALUATION PLAN

A finely tuned evaluation plan is necessary for the credibility of the plan and must state which performance standards will give the plan direction. The performance standards can be a qualitative statement of what the results should be or a quantitative measure. If possible, use both. The key question in determining the desired standard is to ask what you, teachers, community members, and/or non-parents will "see" as a result of this action plan? Will a new curriculum be available? What will it be like? What are the desired characteristics? Will a new or revised day care program be in operation? What are the problems of the present one? What needs are not currently being addressed?

In the case of the example used above, the following will help determine evaluation standards. Are new facilities involved? If so, what kind, what size, what are the functions? Are repairs such as painting involved? If so, what colors? New play equipment? What kind? Which brand names? If the project involves construction, the architectural blueprints will serve as the standard for measurement.

STEP 5.0 – MONITORING AND EVALUATING

As principal, it is your job to monitor the implementation of the management plan. Hang the management plan on the wall by your desk so that you can assess progress at a glance. Require regular, but not burdensome, progress reports from those who are in charge of activities and use the KITA principal when needed. Completion of some activities is dependent on completion of others, so those with responsibility for activities must keep their oars in the water.

The management plan is a guide, not a concrete monolith. It can be revised when needed. We find that numerous revisions are necessary to accommodate the occurrence of unplanned events. There is more than one way to arrive at a destination. The key is to keep on target.

Evaluation should be a breeze if the performance standards are well-defined. We suggest that the project manager, the principal, conduct the evaluation and share it with the committee for critique. They will have their own perspectives which will frequently benefit the evaluation. Surveys such as those presented in Appendix D are very helpful in gaining community members' evaluations of the school. They can be easily revised for each school.

Develop this plan and share the responsibilities with the staff and community. Maintaining their involvement is a fundamental ingredient in MBWA and is key to the success of the plan. The school administrator is ultimately responsible for the outcomes, so use all the resources available: the school staff, community members, central office staff and material resources, and the businesses in the school district.

It's time to go to the media again. Show them the great work you and your school staff and community have done. Don't brag, just tell them what you have accomplished and the plans that lay ahead. Remember what Dizzy Dean said, "It ain't bragging when you can do it." You haven't done it all yet, but you have completed the planning effort. Let the public know about it.

REFERENCES

ALTBACK, P. "Underfunded and 'Oversold,'" *Education Week*. p. 24 (Oct. 1986).

AQUILA, F. D. and J. Galovic. "The Principal as Change Agent—Encouraging Teachers to Adopt Change," *NASSP Bull.*, 72:50+ (March 1988).

BENNETT, W. "Text of Secretary Bennett's 'James Madison High School,'" *Education Week*, pp. 27–30 (January 13, 1988).

BLUMBERG, A. *School Administration as a Craft*. New York:Allyn & Bacon (1989).

BOSSERT, S., S. Dwyer, and G. Lee. "The Instructional Management Role of the Principal," *Educational Administration Quarterly*, 18(3):34–64 (1982).

BRANDT, R. "On School Improvement: A Conversation with Ronald Edmonds," *Educational Leadership*, 40(3):31–35 (1982).

BROOKOVER, W. and L. Lezotte. "Changes in School Characteristics Coincident with Changes in School Achievement," East Lansing:Institute for Research on Teaching, Michigan State University (1979).

BURDIN, J. L. ed. *School Leadership: A Contemporary Reader*. Athens, OH:Sage (1988).

CAMPBELL, R. F., et al. *A History of Thought and Practice in Educational Administration*. Columbia University:Teachers College Press (1987).

DARESCH, J. C. *Supervision as a ProActive Process*. New York:Longman, Inc. (1989).

DEROCHE, E. F. *An Administrator's Guide for Evaluating Programs and Personnel: An Effective Schools Approach*, 2nd edition. Massachusetts:Allyn and Bacon (1988).

EDMONDS, R. "Some Schools Work and More Can," *Social Policy*, 9(2):28–32 (1979).

GALLUP, A. M. and D. L. Clark. "The 19th Gallup Poll of the Public's Attitudes Toward the Public Schools," *Phi Delta Kappan*, pp. 17–30 (Sept. 1987).

GORTON, R. *School Leadership and Administrators: Important Concepts, Case Studies and Simulations*. Dubuque, IA:William C. Brown (1987).

KAUFFMAN, R. *Planning Educational Systems*. Lancaster, PA:Technomic Pub. Co., Inc. (1988).

LANE, J. J. and H. J. Walberg, eds. *Effective School Leadership: Policy and Process*. Berkeley:McCutchan (1987).

LIEBERMAN, A. "Expanding the Leadership Team," *Educ. Leadership*, 445:4–8 (Fall 1988).

LIPSITZ, J. *Successful School for Young Adolescents*. New Brunswick, NJ:Transaction (1984).

MAEROFF, G. I. "A Blueprint for Empowering Teachers," *Phi Delta Kappan*, 69:472–477 (March 1988).

ORNSTEIN, A. "How do Educators Meet the Needs of Society? How Are Education's Aims Determined," *NASSP Bulletin*, pp. 36–47 (May 1985).

PETERS, T. and R. Waterman. *In Search of Excellence*. New York:Warner Books (1982).

ROBINSON, G. "Effective Schools Research: A Guide to School Improvement," Educational Research Service, Inc. (Feb. 1985).

ROSE, M. "Sharing Knowledge, Developing Skills," *Am. Teach.*, pp. 72–73 (March 1988).

RUMELT, R. "Strategy, Structure and Economic Performance," Doctoral Dissertation, Graduate School of Business Administration, Harvard University (1974).

RUTHERFORD, W. L. "School Principals as Effective Leaders," *Phi Delta Kappan*, 67(1):31–34 (1985).

STIMSON, T. D. and R. P. Appelbaum. "Empowering Teachers: Do Principals Have the Power?" *Phi Delta Kappan*, 70:313–316 (December 1988).

VANDEBERGHE, R. "The Principal as Maker of a Local Innovation Policy: Linking Research to Practice," *J. Res. Dev. Educ.*, 2:69–79 (Fall 1988).

VAN DER VEGT, R. and H. Knit. "The Role of the Principal in School Improvement: Steering Functions for Implementation at the School Level," *J. Res. Dev. Educ.*, 22:60–68 (Fall 1988).

WAYSON, W. W., C. Achilles, G. S. Pinnell, M. N. Lintz, L. N. Carol and L. Cunningham. *Handbook for Developing Public Confidence in Schools*. Bloomington, IN:Phi Delta Kappa Commission for Developing Public Confidence in Schools, Phi Delta Kappa Foundation (1988).

ZIRKEL, P. A. and I. B. Bluckman. "Is Your School a Public Forum?" *Principal*, 68:59–60+ (November 1988).

CHAPTER
IV

Promoting the Improvement Ethic

TEACHERS AS LEARNERS

ENSURING that *only* excellent teachers have contact with students is the school administrator's most important role. That's the bottom line. We are in this business to educate young people, and teachers are the most influential factor in the educational process. Other variables, socioeconomic status and locus of control, account for a great deal of variance in test scores but are outside educators' span of control (Coleman, Campbell, Hobson, McParland, Mood, Weinfeld, and York, 1966; Freedle and Kostin, 1987; Olmedo, 1981; and Jencks, 1972). Educators can influence the quality of teaching, however, and this is where we must invest the majority of our energy and efforts. Helping teachers do a great job for young people through robust, cutting edge professional development programs is what this chapter is about.

Professional development means helping teachers further enhance their understanding of students and their teaching skills. Professional development is crucial to every school and every staff member. Professional development programs help excellent teachers stay on the cutting edge and help less than excellent teachers improve their skills. Principals and superintendents should strongly encourage training and seek commitment from all staff members to engage in a minimum of thirty-five hours of training per year. Encouragement in the form of cheerleading alone won't do the job. In addition to offering high quality programs, helping financially to pay trainers, funding transportation to conferences, and compensating teachers for their time is a necessity. This goes for administrators, teachers, aides, and custo-dians—all staff members. Training for teachers is addressed in this chapter, but the principles are applicable to any group.

Research has demonstrated that school leaders must play an active role in initiating, guiding, and supporting professional de-velopment if it is to succeed (Sarason, 1972). McKibbin and Joyce (1980) furthered this notion and supported the value of a school climate characterized by an active, upbeat social climate where learning opportunities are compelling, when they found that such an environment transformed teachers who were normally passive consumers into active learners. The MBWA style of being out and about, inquiring, watching, listening, and helping is gaining popularity. Principals of the early 1960s served primar-ily as "gatekeepers." This role entailed such functions as approv-ing ideas, preparing proposals, securing funds, and general management. Today's principal is frequently in the role of change agent. The MBWA change agent promotes ideas as well as ap-proving them, seeks commitment to training, conducts training, receives training, and constantly communicates with teachers about training. He demonstrates its importance through deeds and action.

Educational administrators are in luck because quality profes-sional development programs attract teachers with the force of gravity. The reason for this attraction lies in the reasons the vast majority of teachers are teachers—to help young people learn. That's it, plain and simple. As a learned reader you may ask why we are convinced that this altruistic reason, and not money and fringe benefits, plays the biggest role in attracting teachers. Although this is not and is not intended to be a research-laden book, it is important to provide some of the research evidence which supports this contention. A very informal discussion of the research literature on this topic follows.

MOTIVES FOR TEACHING

People in the "helping professions," as opposed to those in sales and industry, typically espouse altruistic reasons for doing their job, and teaching illustrates this most dramatically. First, why do teachers enter teaching?

Dan Lortie's (1975) sociological study of teachers and a recent review of his work (Kottkamp, Provenzo, and Cohn, 1986) found that the psychic rewards in working with young people and a desire to render service were the most widespread motives for teaching. Other reasons included positive personal experiences with school, interest in a particular subject area, the nine-month work year, and the job security traditionally associated with teaching. The California Roundtable on Educational Opportunities (1983) found that the reasons for entering teaching could be grouped into two categories: (1) altruistic motives–the desire to serve and work with young people and (2) practical motives–decent salaries, job security, time off in the summer, and some upward mobility. They reported that educational altruism (the desire to work with young people) is the strongest motive for undertaking a teaching career. Surveys by the National Education Association in 1971, 1976, and 1981 revealed similar results; approximately 70 percent of the teachers surveyed named educational altruism as the primary reason for becoming a teacher, with interests in a subject area and the significance of teaching and education in society following in importance. Studies by Fruth (1982), Kane (1989), Griffin and Tantiwong (1989), and Joseph and Green (1986) support the finding that the most powerful motivational force for attracting teachers is "working with students." In summary, the number one goal for teachers is straightforward and most altruistic–"to help young people learn."

The reasons for teachers staying in the profession are quite similar. The Wisconsin study found the altruistic motive, "working with students," to be the most important reason for staying in teaching with practical motives such as the work schedule and job security being second in importance. In a 1986 study, C. Emily Feistritzer (1986) asked a random sample of teachers to identify those job factors most important to them. The factor most frequently identified was "chance to use my mind and abilities" and the second, by only one percentage point, was "chance to work with young people and see them develop." A recent study by Azumi and Lerman (1987) found that teachers in Newark, a large urban district, ranked "having input into policymaking and participating in educational decision making" as their most satisfying professional activity. In summary, just as the initial motivation for entering the field is altruistic in nature, so are the reasons for staying.

Factors which serve as motivators for teachers on the job are also similar. Sergiovanni's (1967) study of teachers revealed the following as the most powerful motivators for teachers.

ACHIEVEMENT–successfully completing a job, developing a solution to a problem, and seeing the results of one's work.

RECOGNITION–experiencing an act of recognition from any of a variety of sources: principal, student, parent, peer, etc.

RESPONSIBILITY–being given responsibility for work without supervision or being given responsibility for the work of others.

These are not isolated results. Savage (1971), Wickstrom (1967), and Schmidt (1976) reported similar findings with both teachers and administrators. Lortie, in the study mentioned earlier, indicated that teachers consistently rated altruistic rewards such as "knowing I have reached students and they have learned" as more important than other rewards, particularly extrinsic rewards. Pastor and Erlandson (1982) found that the strongest motivators for teachers were higher-order needs such as those stated by Sergiovanni.

These reasons for entering and staying in teaching and the job factors most important to teachers set teachers apart from nearly all other professions. Tom Peters (1987, p. 174) has highlighted the sales force at Nordstroms as being caring and truly dedicated as evidenced by the attention and care they give customers. Based on popular opinion, this is an accurate statement. However, the more important question is why are the salespeople so attentive and caring? The answer is far different from the answer to the same question about teachers. Teachers are in the teaching profession because they want to work with young people and are internally motivated to help them learn. The sales force at Nordstroms or any other clothing store are not there because their main goal in life is to sell clothes or see to it that people are well-dressed. They are there to earn a living and are motivated to do a good job by slick motivational programs which focus on external rewards such as money.

THE QUALITY LOOK IN PROFESSIONAL DEVELOPMENT PROGRAMS

The bad news is that the research base for professional training and development is sparse. In 1980, Lawrence and Harrison reported that of over 6,000 references on staff development programs, only 159 contained quantitative data, and only 59 of those contained sufficient data to be used in a meta-analysis (Lawrence and Harrison, 1980). The good news is that high-quality studies have been completed since that offer considerable direction for formulating and running professional development programs.

Recent efforts have been directed to training teachers using teaching-effectiveness research. Sparks' (1983) review of this literature highlights the following ten findings on the delivery of professional training.

(1) Select content that has been verified by research to improve student achievement.

(2) Create a context of acceptance by involving teachers in decision making and providing both logistical and psychological administrative support.

(3) Conduct training sessions two or three weeks apart.

(4) Include presentation, demonstration, practice, and feedback as workshop activities.

(5) During training sessions provide opportunities for small group discussions of the application of new practices and sharing of ideas and concerns about effective instruction.

(6) Between workshops, encourage teachers to visit each other's classrooms, preferably with a simple, objective, student-centered observation instrument. Provide opportunities for discussions of the observation.

(7) Develop in teachers a philosophical acceptance of the new practices by presenting research and a rationale for the effectiveness of the technique. Allow teachers to express doubts about or objections to the recommended methods in small groups. Let the other teachers convince the resisting teacher of the usefulness of the practices through "testimonies" of their use and effectiveness.

(8) Lower teachers' perceptions of the cost of adopting a new practice through detailed discussions of the "nuts and bolts" of using the technique and through teachers sharing experiences with the technique.

(9) Help teachers grow in their self-confidence and competence by encouraging them to try only one or two new practices after each workshop. Diagnosis of teacher strengths and

weaknesses can help the trainer suggest changes that are likely to be successful and thus reinforce future efforts to change.

(10) For teaching practices that require very complex thinking skills, plan to take more time, provide more practice, and consider activities that develop conceptual flexibility.

These findings are echoed and expanded by Little (1984) who stresses the importance of teacher participation in program planning and development, collegiality, and basing program content on research on effective teaching. Little's research included two well-designed programs for teams of teachers which met these requirements. Initially, teachers from both programs were enthusiastic about the training. But after three years teachers from only one program were continuing to use the recommended instructional practices. Why? There are no firm answers, but there is a firm caution: don't be deceived by the illusion of improvement, e.g., initial enthusiasm.

Little (1984) concluded that professional training programs are most influential when they:

(1) Ensure collaboration adequate to produce shared understanding, shared investment, thoughtful development, and the fair, rigorous test of selected ideas

(2) Require collective participation in training and implementation

(3) Are focused on crucial problems of curriculum and instruction

(4) Are conducted often enough and long enough to ensure progressive gains in knowledge, skill, and confidence

(5) Are congruent and contribute to professional habits and norms of collegiality and experimentation

In a comprehensive survey of successful staff development programs, Van Tulder and Veenman (1989) identified the following components of effective training programs.

(1) Objectives focus on teaching skills supported by research. Knowledge, insight, and attitude should not be neglected but should not be the major focus of the training.

(2) Training should be practical and concrete.

(3) The theoretical basis or description of the skills to be learned should be provided.

(4) Skills to be learned should be modeled by experts.

(5) Practice should take place in simulated and classroom settings.

(6) Structured and open-ended feedback (information) about performance should be provided frequently.

(7) Coaching for application (i.e., hands-on support, in-classroom assistance) should be provided.

Only 80% of staff development programs contain three of the required components, and only a few contain all seven. Less than 10% of the programs are based on a long-term plan at the school level, utilize coaching, or provide systematic feedback.

The list of characteristics identified by Sparks (1983), Little (1984), and van Tulder and Veenman (1989) appear diverse, but share the following points: skills supported by research, modeling, systematic feedback regarding performance, coaching, collaboration and participation among all those involved, and practicality.

Principals must not only ensure that staff development programs contain key characteristics; they must adopt a management style conducive to successful implementation. Simply listing characteristics common to successful programs is somewhat analogous to piling all the parts to a Porsche and expecting them to form the car and run. It won't happen. Likewise, principals must develop and model a philosophy and related management style to activate program components into a successful program. Van der Vegt and Knip (1987) have helped by identifying the following management characteristics common to principals who have developed and implemented successful programs:

- establish and clarify goals
- give direction for accomplishing the goals
- provide assistance and support
- restrict latitude, i.e., keep everyone on track

In essence, principals in schools with successful programs are characterized as "instructional leaders" (Duke, 1987).

TWO PURPOSES OF PROFESSIONAL DEVELOPMENT PROGRAMS

There are essentially two purposes for professional development programs within the overall purpose of helping teachers do a better job of helping young people learn.

1. *Quality Control.* The principal is responsible for insuring that quality instruction is taking place in each classroom. To do so the principal must practice MBWA in a planned, purposeful manner. The MBWA route should take you into each classroom at least twice a week, tours of the school grounds at least twice a week, and talking with staff and students every day. Be sure to schedule these MBWA activities on your calendar. Determining answers to the following questions modified from Sergiovanni's work (1987, p. 152) will help put purpose in MBWA wanderings:

- What is actually going on in the classroom?
- Do the activities correspond to the objectives?
- What is the teacher and what are the students actually doing?
- What are the actual learning objectives and outcomes? Is there a match?
- What ought to be going on in these classrooms given the school's mission statement and goals, knowledge of how youngsters learn, and understanding of the structure of the subject matter to be taught?
- What do the activities taking place mean to the teachers, other staff, and students?
- Is the teacher using appropriate instructional strategies? Are they being used properly?
- What are the personal meanings that students accumulate regardless of teacher intents?
- How do the teachers' and your interpretations of the reality of teaching differ? How are they the same?
- What actions should be taken to bring about even more in-depth understanding of the teaching and learning going on in the school?
- What can be done to develop a better congruence between our actions and beliefs?

MBWA is obviously crucial to learning the answers to any of these questions, and it is no surprise that MBWA, or practicing supervision in classrooms, is a key characteristic of effective schools. Quality control and teacher improvement must drive the supervisory program and provide the backbone for determining the content and form of professional development programs. Perhaps even more important is the unspoken powerful message it communicates to the staff–"What you do is important; you are important; teaching and learning are the most important aspects of my job, and spending time in your classroom, watching and helping, is the best way to communicate my commitment to you."

2. *Teacher Motivation.* Building and nurturing motivation and commitment to teaching, to the school's overall purposes, and to the evolution of the school's educational mission is seldom considered a formal responsibility of administrators, although this belief is increasing. Overwhelming evidence exists that "knowledge of results" is a crucial ingredient in increasing a person's motivation to work and in building commitment and loyalty to one's job (Hackman and Oldman, 1975, 1976 and 1980). Feedback need not occur only during formal post-evaluation conferences. MBWA offers ideal opportunities for providing feedback. When the focus of the wander has been determined, it becomes easy to give feedback. The focus is important because it gives the administrator *specific* information to feed back to the staff member such as:

- "I liked the direct instruction technique you used with the reading group today, it was well-suited to the lesson and you did it well."
- "Nice job handling the spat between the two boys this morning; the conflict management skills you picked up last month really paid off."

Specificity is key. It doesn't take a dolt, dullard, or the feeble-minded lummox long to realize that trite statements such as "great job" and "hey, that was terrific" sound false and empty and don't provide direction. Feedback is important and must be specific before it can have motivational effects.

Professional development activities also provide powerful mechanisms for further motivating teachers. Wright (1985) has demonstrated that teachers are highly motivated by professional activities which stress intrinsic values as opposed to extrinsic motivators. Frase's (1989) research has shown evidence that opportunities to participate in professional training programs lead to increased recognition from peers and increased internal motivation.

So much for theory, professional development by definition is a major responsibility for administrators at all levels. It helps teachers achieve their number one goal of helping young people learn, fulfills the public schools' responsibility to the community, and rejuvenates and further enhances teachers' motivation to do their very best job possible. Professional development and feedback offer opportunities for teachers, or any staff member, to experience achievement, responsibility, and recognition, three powerful motivational factors for teachers.

THE WHAT OF PROFESSIONAL DEVELOPMENT: CONTENT

Determining the content and form of professional development programs must not be a hit and miss routine. Teachers who haphazardly determine the content and lessons for their students are not respected. The same is true for principals and superintendents who offer in-service training on a seemingly random basis.

CONCEPTUAL CONSIDERATIONS

How can content for a professional development program be conceptualized? Rubin (1975, p. 44) offers four substance areas he believes can be improved through professional development.

The Teacher's Sense of Purpose

Sense of purpose and perception of students form the value base, beliefs, and assumptions which become the basis for making decisions about classroom organization, teaching, and interacting with students. In other words, a principal concerned about a teacher's excessive focus on drill and rote practice must address the teacher's sense of purpose and perception of students. Offering training activities on alternative instructional techniques may address the symptom, but not the problem.

The Teacher's Perception of Students

The desire to educate students is key to a successful professional career in education. Teachers are no longer required to pledge their *love* of children as a sign of commitment to the mission of the organization. Nevertheless, educators must continually strive to do the best job possible for the young people in their care. Young people are our reason for being in education; without them there would be no need for teachers or principals.

The Teacher's Knowledge of Subject Matter

The necessity of possessing a strong command of the subject matter is requisite to the ability to expand student's grasp and thinking about the subject. An intimate knowledge of subject matter is frequently the difference between mediocre and mastery teaching. As Louis Rubin (1975, p. 47) stated

> When teachers are genuinely knowledgeable, when they know their subject well enough to discriminate between the seminal ideas and the secondary matter, when they go beyond what is in the textbook, the quality of pedagogy becomes extraordinarily impressive.

The Teacher's Mastery of Technique

Both content and technique are important, and the argument as to which is more important has raged on for many years. The facts seem obvious. One cannot teach something without knowing the content, but that is not enough. Possessing mastery of instructional techniques, classroom management, and other basic skills allows effective delivery of content. All four of Ruben's substance areas are requisite to effective instruction and must be integral parts of any professional development program.

Sergiovanni (1987, p. 159) combines these teaching substance areas with professional development competence areas in Figure 4.1 and provides a system of viewing teachers' competency levels and attitudes toward professional commitment. The three areas are KNOWS HOW/CAN DO, WILL DO, and WILL GROW. Each is defined in Figure 4.1.

Substance Areas	Competency Areas		
	Knows How/Can Do?	Will Do?	Will Grow?
Purpose			
Students			
Subject Matter			
Teaching Techniques			

FIGURE 4.1 Professional growth matrix. Printed with permission from Sergiovanni, T. J. *The Principalship: A Reflective Practice Perspective.* Copyright © 1987 by Allyn and Bacon, Inc.

(1) **Knows How/Can Do:** Teachers must know how to do their jobs and have the professional responsibility to keep their skills sharp. But knowing is not enough; teachers must be able to demonstrate effective application of their content knowledge.

(2) **Will Do:** Teachers can cook up a good lesson when required to do so. The more important question is whether they "will do" the job to the best of their ability on a consistent basis and of their own volition, without the principal present.

(3) **Will Grow:** Professional development is the "will grow" competency area. Professional growth and improvement is a basic credo of any profession, and teaching requires even more professional integrity than other professions such as physicians and lawyers since their income is to a large extent based on performance and is highly competitive. Teachers are organizational professionals whose performance is not open, in most cases, to public scrutiny and whose performance has long been thought to be difficult to measure. This attitude is changing and professional development is seen as a key element to increasing respect for the profession.

In sum, professional development addresses the extent to which teachers demonstrate their skills and attitudes in regard to Know How/Can Do, Will Do, and Will Grow questions as they relate to the purpose, students, subject matter, and teaching techniques substance areas.

The following are examples of questions which can be asked for each of the competency areas. The substance area used in these examples is "teaching techniques." Is the teacher knowledgeable about a wide variety of instructional techniques and models such as the essential elements of instruction, direct instruction, lecturing, appropriate practice, and knowledge of results? Can the teacher demonstrate these? Does the teacher demonstrate use of these skills when appropriate (properly match the technique with the situation). Are they used consistently over a sustained period of time? Does the teacher demonstrate the desire to grow professionally? Does the teacher voluntarily engage in an adequate number of professional growth activities which expand his/her professionalism? Do the teachers accept and benefit from constructive criticism?

Answering questions such as these for each of the teaching substance areas offers much grist for the professional development mill and will prevent oversight of one or more competency areas and exclusion of either content or teaching attitudes.

TECHNIQUES FOR DETERMINING CONTENT

Information gained from the matrix presented in Figure 4.1 can be used as one piece of the puzzle for determining the topics to be addressed in in-service workshops and conferences. Other pieces include evaluators' assessments, self-assessment surveys, and suggestions from research. We will start with the latter.

Among the topics addressed in training programs provided over the past three years, it is likely that the following would be identified: Essential Elements of Instruction, Mastery Learning, Direct Instruction, TESA, and cooperative learning. All of these are popular and certainly offer valuable teaching skills. The question is whether teachers are ready for these lessons. Do other skills serve as prerequisites? If so, are the prerequisite skills in place? Brophy (1979, 1982) contends that research over the past fifteen years suggests that some skills are requisite to others and that there is a definite order in which teacher skills should be presented. Training should always be based on need, but in general, teacher training should start with *quantity* of time spent learning and progress to *quality* of time spent learning. The sequence of topics is provided in Figure 4.2.

1	2	3	4	5	6
Time on Task	Behavior Management/ Discipline	Classroom Management/ Grouping	Instructional Sequence/ Lesson Design	Teacher Expectations Differential Treatment of Students	Program Quality: Effects on Students

Quantity of Time Spent Learning	⟶	Quality of Time Spent Learning

FIGURE 4.2 Research-based sequence for professional development.

The authors' MBWA observations support this assertion. Before teachers can effectively use advanced instructional techniques, they must first be able to manage the classroom and maintain discipline. Before teachers can consider the differential treatment of students in the instructional setting, the instructional sequence must first be set and thoroughly understood. This sequence represents another piece in the puzzle for determining topics to be included in the professional development program.

The sequence of training topics presented above is particularly useful in programming training sessions for relatively new teachers to the profession. For experienced staff, however, specific information about competencies is also needed. Three techniques for making this assessment are provided below.

MBWA Anecdotes

As stated numerous times, MBWA must have a purpose. The questions previously addressed for MBWA provide an effective MBWA focus for determining staff training needs. Keep these topics and questions in mind as you visit classrooms, visit with teachers in the lounge, listen to teacher conversations, and discuss teacher training needs. Creative ideas will come from these efforts if you empower teachers to select and determine their training needs. Indeed, determining training topics and the format for training must sometimes be left to the administrator, but sharing the power will pay dividends in creative ideas. The technique which follows is a paper/pencil means of gathering teacher perceptions about their professional development training needs.

Broad-Based Assessment

This procedure is called broad-based because it assesses both perceived competency and interest in each of the training topics.

Teachers are asked to do the rating and averages are determined for each training topic. The lower the average, the lower the perceived competency. The opposite is true for the interest in training. When the averages are complete, compare the perceived competency with the interest in training. The first programs to be developed should be those with the lowest ratings in perceived need and interest in training. Other factors must also be considered. First, information gained from MBWA must be taken into account; second, the sequence of training topics by Brophy must be considered to insure continuity; and third, the administrator must rely on administrative perceptions and observations about training needs.

It is permissible to form a committee to develop the instrument. Empowering teachers to be responsible for activities which affect them has been suggested numerous times in this book. Don't overdo it. Doing so will result in the group suspecting that you either can't make a decision or you are too lazy. If the administra-

Instructor Skill | Degree of Perceived Competency | Interest

	Expertise in: Experienced & can serve as consultant	Worked with: Have experience but not qualified as consultant	Knowledge of: Definition only	No Knowledge of: No knowledge to knowledge of simple definition only	Very much desire training	Somewhat desire training	Do not desire training
	4	3	2	1	1	2	3
Diagnosis of Learning Problems							
Classroom Management Conferencing with Parents							

tor is highly trusted and if the climate is right, it may be permissible to form the instrument, get feedback from teachers, distribute it for completion, and report the results. A sample list of assessment items is presented in Appendix E.

Administrative Judgements

Administrators are responsible for their schools, the teachers in them, and the quality of teaching taking place. Administrators are also obligated to attain and maintain a high level of instructional expertise. With these responsibilities and instructional skills, it is the administrator's responsibility to evaluate teaching. Observing and being observed and giving and getting feedback about one's work in the classroom are the most powerful tools for instructional improvement and professional recognition. Stories of principals completing evaluations without ever setting foot in the teacher's classroom are all too common, far more sad than humorous, and all too often true. A recent study revealed that 26 percent of teachers are never observed and an additional 27 percent are observed only once a year (Huddle, 1985). Valid evaluations require instructional expertise and multiple classroom observations of a minimum of forty-five minutes. The acid test of any administrator's evaluations is whether or not the full range of rating is used, i.e., were all teachers rated good-to-great on all criteria or were some teachers rated "poor" or "unacceptable," at least on some criteria? If all teachers were rated good-to-great, as was the case in thirty-four Pennsylvania school districts (Langlois and Colarusso, 1988), the tough, yet honest decisions are not being made and the teaching profession and students are not being treated fairly. Receipt of accurate and constructive recommendations for improvement is not a disgrace. Everyone has room for improvement. In fact, teachers reserve their highest approval rating for observations/evaluation options that were more extensive and demanding than those which their administrators were actually using (Bird and Little, 1986). There is strong reason to believe that teachers support rigorous observation procedures that can hold teachers accountable for the practices, when those same practices also support them and provide them recognition for their work in the classroom (Bird and Little, 1986). Ignoring the inadequacies and pretending that they do not exist is a disgrace to all teachers and administrators.

Pointing out, with a sense of conviction, how a teacher can improve a lesson will serve to further enhance your esteem in the eyes of the teacher and ultimately contribute to enhancing the public's esteem of the teaching profession.

A field-tested teacher evaluation instrument is presented in Appendix F for your use. The strengths of the instrument are: (1) all teacher behaviors/criteria are validated by the fact that each has a base in research which links the behavior to teacher effectiveness and student achievement; (2) the ratings range from inadequate to professionally competent which allows superior ratings or inadequate ratings for use in helping teachers improve or ultimately dismissing teachers who fail to reach minimum standards; and (3) requires the evaluator to justify the rating in narrative form. The latter is very important and helps prevent the natural tendency to assign the same rating to all teachers.

A teacher observation instrument does not exist in isolation and is one part of the total teacher evaluation process. The eight steps to a total evaluation process are presented and discussed below.

EVALUATION PROCESS

Orientation
Self-Evaluation
Planning Conference
Pre-Observation Report (Conference Optional)
Formal Observations
Post-Observation Feedback Conference
Supporting Data
Summative Evaluation

Orientation: This is the time for orienting the teacher to the evaluation process (instruments, timelines, and quality expectations), philosophy, and "annual instructional focus."

Self-evaluation: The self-evaluation provides the teacher an opportunity to review and reflect upon the district's adopted performance areas and the annual instructional focus. The purpose of the self-evaluation is to establish a mind-set for the evaluation process and to provide direction toward areas of concern or interest. It is interesting to note that only 33 percent of the districts in the nation require teachers to conduct self-evaluations.

Planning Conference: This conference provides an opportunity for the evaluator and teacher to do the following:

(1) Review the teacher's self-evaluation and performance record
(2) Review professional growth goals and progress toward their accomplishment
(3) Establish new professional growth plans or goals, if needed
(4) Address questions or concerns related to the evaluation process

Pre-Observation Report:

(1) At this stage the teacher and evaluator establish the date, time, and place of the observation (if first observation) and post-conference.
(2) The teacher provides the evaluator a completed pre-observation report and lesson plans or other pertinent material the evaluator or teacher chooses. Either party must be able to call a conference to discuss the pre-observation report.

Formal Observations: Formal observations should cover an entire lesson or a minimum of forty-five minutes. A forty-five-minute observation may appear too long and serve to intimidate teachers. This depends on the principal's trust level with the teacher. Shorter observations may make the teacher feel more comfortable but cannot possibly add up to a mechanism for the improvement of teaching, the primary goal of evaluation observations. In reality, teachers claim that they do not begin to have faith in an observer's grasp of their teaching in less than three visits of adequate length (Bird and Little, 1986). Shorter supplementary observations are also desirable and should be part of the MBWA plan just as with the longer observations. There is a strong sentiment for announcing all evaluation visits. This practice is satisfactory for the formal observation of the year, but others should not be announced. As stated in the discussion of the "will do" teacher competency area presented in Figure 4.1, it is crucial that teachers do a good job consistently and over a sustained period of time. Pre-announcing each visit will prohibit accurate assessment of the "will do" dimension.

Post-Observation Conference: This conference should be held soon after the observation and is the time for the evaluator and teacher to discuss the lesson, the evaluator's findings, and the teacher's perceptions.

Supporting Data: This is the teacher's opportunity to submit information for the evaluator's consideration prior to completion of the summative evaluation report: student data collected by the teacher or evaluator; portfolios of work samples such as summaries of professional meetings and conferences attended, student grade reports, memoranda, letters, lesson plans, student work samples, tests and related analyses; etc. Informal MBWA observations should also be conducted during this time. Prior to the summative evaluation, the teacher must be given the opportunity to respond to data or anecdotal records which result from the informal observations or commendations or complaints which occur after the formal observation and before the summative evaluation.

Summative Evaluation: The summative evaluation consists of a written report by the evaluator and a conference to review the report and discuss ideas for the growth plan. Teachers should be given the opportunity to submit a written response to the summative evaluation report for inclusion in the teacher's personnel file.

Teacher evaluation and observation conducted as part of the MBWA plan, anecdotal notes taken during MBWA activities, and information gained from assessment instruments are rich sources of data for determining professional development programs. Professional growth programs are not an end in themselves. They are important to the extent that they insure that *only highly qualified teachers are in contact with students.*

PRINCIPAL AS LEARNER:
DEMONSTRATING THE IMPROVEMENT ETHIC

The third most frequently cited reason by teachers for leaving the profession is lack of respect for administrators' abilities. This hits hard! The idea that good teachers leave due to lack of respect for administrators' abilities is humiliating and, based on the author's experience, frequently true. The following are five of the most irritating supervisory behaviors.

(1) Never or rarely compliments me on a job well done
(2) Acts as if he knows it all
(3) Procrastinates on problems

(4) Gives impractical suggestions regarding instruction and classroom management

(5) Passes the buck

These common sources of irritation closely match the author's experience and these sources tend to reflect lack of feedback, lack of confidence, and lack of expertise in classroom management and instruction.

It is true that some teachers may use administrative shortcomings as a scapegoat to cover their own reasons of inadequacy. It also may be true that the administrator made a good decision the teacher did not like. These are easily dismissed. But the fact is that professional development applies to all staff, including administrators. Just qualifying for a teaching certificate does not mean that a teacher is a great or even adequate teacher, and qualifying for an administrative certificate does not guarantee that the administrator will be adequate or great. Actively engaging in professional development will bring improvement and new heights of respect from teachers, parents, other administrators, and *self*. For the successful leader, awareness of a need for improvement is a beginning, the springboard of hope (Bennis and Nanus, 1985).

Two techniques for determining topics to be included in a professional development plan are discussed below.

ADMINISTRATOR ASSESSMENT CENTERS AND OTHER TRAINING PROGRAMS

Assessment centers are currently being operated by professional associations such as American Association of School Administrators and National Association of Secondary School Principals. Assessment centers consist of a standardized evaluation of behavior based on multiple inputs. Trained observers and techniques are used to make judgements about administrative behavior in simulations. Behavioral dimensions such as the following are assessed: (1) personal qualities, (2) interpersonal skills, (3) administrative skills, and (4) communication skills. These areas represent the "people skills" and basic managerial skills which are a must for success in any administrative position. Content skills are not typically addressed in assessment center programs. If interested in pursuing activity in an assessment center, contact your county or state educational associations for information. These programs are sometimes expensive—$400–$1,000, but they provide excellent analyses of administrative strengths and weaknesses in the people skills, analytical skills, leadership, planning and organizing, stress tolerance, and decision making, among others.

Other high quality training programs are provided through the Harvard Principals' Center, Vanderbilt University two-week summer institute, and the Far West Laboratory's Peer-Assisted Leadership Program.

FEEDBACK FROM TEACHERS, STAFF, AND SUPERVISORS

The people you work with on a daily basis can provide insight into personal strengths and weaknesses. This need not be a threatening endeavor; it should be fun, informative and challenging. Let your staff (teachers, secretaries, custodians, etc.) know that you are interested in doing the very best job possible. Their help will be of great assistance in achieving this end. Two instruments are provided for use in gathering this information. The first is provided below and was also presented in Chapter I. It is brief, straightforward, and open-ended, while the second is longer and structured. The second (see Appendix I) is modified from Slezak (1984, p. 116). An advantage of the first is that it allows the staff member to state concerns and compliments in their own words and avoids the restrictions of rating preset criteria or topics. The disadvantage is that some may not feel comfortable in using their handwriting in that their response will not be anonymous. The advantage of the second is that responses are anonymous and topics can be predetermined. Use of both or a combination of both is suggested. In addition, the second instrument can be completed by teachers, the administrator, and by supervisors of the administrator. Comparison of these ratings typically reveals broad discrepancies which offer insight and clues to our performance and how others perceive us. This information gives direction for professional improvement programs.

ADMINISTRATOR FEEDBACK FORM

Directions

Please write/type your response to each of the following. The information provided on this form will be used with other information in building my professional development plan for the year. All information will be strictly confidential.

To: _____   **From:** _____   **(optional)**

1. Our principal's greatest strength is—
2. Our principal's greatest weakness is—
3. The thing I appreciate most about our principal is—
4. The thing I would change about our principal is—
5. The biggest problem our school faces is—
6. The real strength of our school is—

The Administrator Skills Inventory presented in Appendix I has not been normed; determining the standard of acceptable performance is up to you. We suggest analyzing the responses, checking them against your ratings, and drawing up a "to be improved" list. The means for improvement are obviously varied and many: readings, training conferences, discussions with significant others, observations of model principals, having qualified others observe you and give feedback, and discussing certain items with your staff. Sometimes the discussion leads to greater understanding of the area to be improved and improves rapport with staff. The important point is that regardless of your score, the school administrator should be looking toward improvement—practicing and modeling the improvement work ethic.

REFERENCES

Azumi, J. and J. Lerman. "Selecting and Rewarding Master Teachers: What Teachers in One District Think," *The Elementary School Journal*, 88(2): 189–201 (1987).

Bennet, M. "Classroom Observations (Ways to Eliminate Teacher Isolation)," *Thrust*, 18:30–31 (October 1988).

Bird, T. and J. Little. "Instructional Leadership 'Close to the Classroom' in Secondary Schools," in *Leading and Managing Change*, pp. 113–138 (1986).

Coleman, J., E. Campbell, C. Hobson, J. McParland, Mood, F. Weinfeld and R. York. *Equality of Educational Opportunity*. Washington, D.C.:United States Printing Office, OE-38001.

Daresch, J. C. *Supervision as a ProActive Process*. New York:Longman, Inc. (1989).

Duke, D. *School Leadership and Instructional Improvement*. New York:Random House.

Feistritzer, C. E. *Profile of Teachers in the U.S.* Washington, D.C.:National Center for Education Information (1986).

FRASE, L. "Assessing the Effects of Intrinsic and Extrinsic Rewards on Teacher Recognition and Opportunities for Job Enrichment," Forthcoming, *Journal of Educational Research* (in press).

FREEDLE, R. and I. Kostin. *Semantic and Structural Factors Affecting the Performance of Matched Black and White Examinees on Analogy Items from the Scholastic Aptitude Test.* Princeton:Educational Testing Service (1987).

FRUTH, M. J. et al. "Commitment to Teaching: Teachers' Responses to Organization Incentives," Wisconsin Center for Education Research, University of Wisconsin-Madison (Feb. 1982).

GINSBERG, R. "Principals as Instructional Leaders: An Ailing Panacea," *Educ. Urban Soc.*, 20:276–293 (May 1988).

GRIFFIN, M. and T. Tantiwong. "A Six Year View of Why Women Students Want to Become Teachers," Presented at the Annual Meeting of the American Educational Research Association, San Francisco, CA (1989).

HACKMAN, R. and G. Oldham. "Motivation Through the Design of Work: Test of a Theory," *Organizational Behavior and Human Performance*, 16(2):250–279.

HACKMAN, R., et al. "New Strategy for Job Enrichment," *California Management Review*, 17(4) (1975).

HARRIS, B. M. *In-Service Education for Staff Development.* Allyn & Bacon (1989).

HUDDLE, G. "Teacher Evaluation. How Important for Effective Schools? Eight Lessons from Research," *NASSP Bulletin*, pp. 59–63 (March 1985).

HUGHES et al. "Personality and Motivation Variables in Tomorrow's Teachers: A Center for Excellence," *Education*, 108:393–403 (Spring 1988).

HUNTER, M. C. "Staff Meetings That Produce Staff Development," *Principal*, 67:44–45 (January 1988).

JENCKS, C. S., M. Smith, H. Ackland, M. Bane, D. Cohen, H. Gintis, B. Heyns and Michelson. *Inequality: A Reassessment of the Effect of Family and Schooling in America.* New York:Basic Books (1972).

JOSEPH, P. B. and N. Green. "Perspectives on Reasons for Becoming Teachers," *Journal of Teacher Education.* 37(6):28–33 (1986).

KANE, P. R. "Attraction to Teaching: A Study of Graduating Seniors at Columbia and Barnard College," Presented at the 1989 Annual Meeting of the American Educational Research Association Conference, San Francisco, CA, March 27–31, 1989.

KAUFMAN, R. *Planning Educational Systems.* 2nd ed. Lancaster, PA:Technomic Publishing Co. (1988).

KOTTKAMP, R., E. Provenzo and M. Cohn. "Stability and Change in a Profession: Two Decades of Teacher Attitudes (1964–1984)," *Phi Delta Kappan*, 67(8):559–567 (1986).

LANGLOIS, D. E. and M. R. Colarusso. "Improving Teacher Evaluation," *Educ. Digest.* 54:13–15 (November 1988) or *The Executive Educator*, pp. 32–33 (May 1988).

LAWRENCE, G. and D. Harrison. *Policy Implication of the Research on the Professional Development of Education Personnel. An Analysis of Fifty-Nine Studies.* Washington, D.C.:Feistritzer Publications (1980).

LESOURD, S. J. and M. L. Grady. "Principal Leadership for Instructional Goal Attainment," *Clearing House*, 62:61–64 (October 1988).

LEVINE, S. *Promoting Adult Growth in Schools: The Promise of Professional Development.* Allyn & Bacon (1989).

LITTLE, J. *School Success and Staff Development* (1984).

LORTIE, D. *School Teacher: A Sociological Study.* Chicago:University of Chicago Press (1975).

McKIBBIN, M. and J. Bruce. "Psychological States and Staff Development," *Theory into Practice,* 19:248–255 (Autumn 1980).

National Education Association Surveys (1971, 1976, 1981).

OLMEDO, E. L. "Testing Linguistic Minorities," *American Psychologist.* 36: 1078–1085 (1981).

ORLICH, D. C. *Staff Development: Enhancing Human Potential.* Allyn & Bacon (1989).

PARKEY et al. "A Study of the Relationship Among Teacher Efficacy, Locus of Control, and Stress," *J. Res. Dev. Educ.,* 1:13–22 (Summer 1988).

PASTOR, M. and D. Erlandson. "A Study of Higher Order Need Strength and Job Satisfaction in Secondary Public School Teachers," *The Journal of Educational Administration.* 20(2):172–183 (1982).

PETERS, T. *Thriving on Chaos.* New York:Knopf, p. 174 (1987).

RUBIN, L. "The Case for Staff Development," in *Professional Supervision for Professional Teachers,* T. J. Sergiovanni, ed. Washington, D.C.:Association for Supervision and Curriculum Development, pp. 33–49 (1975).

RYAN, R. L. *The Complete In-service Staff Development Program: A Step-by-Step Manual for School Administrators.* Prentice-Hall (1987).

SARASON, S. *The Culture of the School and the Problem of Change.* Boston:Allyn and Bacon (1971).

SAVAGE, R. M. "A Study of Teacher Satisfaction and Attitudes: Causes and Effects," Dissertation, Auburn Univ. (1967).

SCHMIDT, G. L. "Job Satisfaction Among Secondary School Administrators," *Educational Administration Quarterly,* 12:81–88 (1976).

SCHWARTZ, G. "Voices: The Teacher; We are Not Machines," *Educ. Leadership.* 46:83 (October 1988).

SERGIOVANNI, T. J. "Factors Which Affect Satisfaction and Dissatisfaction of Teachers," *The Journal of Educational Administration,* pp. 66–82 (1967).

SERGIOVANNI, T. *The Principalship: A Reflective Perspective.* Newton, MA:Allyn and Bacon (1987).

SLEZAK, J. *Odyssey to Excellence.* Merritt:San Francisco, p. 386 (1984).

SMITH, S. et al. "Improving the Attractiveness of the L–12 Teaching Profession in California," *California Round Table on Educational Opportunity,* pp. 22–25 (March 1983).

SPARKS, G. "Synthesis of Research on Staff Development for Effective Teaching," *Educational Leadership,* 41(2):71.

THOMSON, S. D. "Troubled Kingdoms, Restless Natives," *Phi Delta Kappan,* 70:371–375 (January 1989).

VAN DER VEGT, R. and J. Knip. "The Role of the Principal in School Improvement: Steering Functions for Implementation at the School Level." Presented at the Annual Meeting of the American Educational Research Association, San Francisco, CA (1989).

VAN TULDER, M. and S. Veenman. "Characteristics of Inservice Activities and their Effects on Educational Change." Presented at the Annual Meeting of the American Educational Research Association, San Francisco, CA (1989).

WICKSTROM, R. A. "An Investigation into Job Satisfaction Among Teachers," Dissertation, Univ. of Oregon (1971).

WRIGHT, R. "Motivation Teacher Involvement in Professional Growth Activities," *The Canadian Administrator*, 24:1–6 (1985).

CHAPTER
V

MBWA: What to Look For

WHAT will be the focus of the "wander"? MBWA is not simply walking about aimlessly. It must be well-planned and purposeful. This chapter addresses "what to look for" to ensure that MBWA time is purposeful and productive. Four major focal points for MBWA are discussed in this chapter: 1) what to look for in classrooms; 2) how to establish an orderly environment through effective discipline; 3) how to stretch your MBWA time in the community; and 4) how to establish a safe and orderly physical environment.

WANDERING THROUGH CLASSROOMS: WHAT TO LOOK FOR

Just being in classrooms will have a positive impact on teachers, but it won't necessarily influence achievement and learning. Wandering into classrooms provides an opportunity to assess instructional effectiveness, diagnose problems, and reinforce good teaching. It doesn't take extensive observations nor elaborate data gathering to identify critical strengths and weaknesses; it does take a well-focused visit.

Use of instructional time is the key. Anderson et al. (1979) report that children are successfully learning only 37 percent of the total time available. The rest of the time, nothing is being taught, students aren't paying attention, or the material is too difficult. Optimizing learning means optimizing: (1) the total time allocated, (2) the time students are engaged on a learning task, and (3) the success rate on engaged tasks. The importance of each of these is illustrated in the following work by Walsh (1985) which relates achievement of basic skills to time.

Units of Time	Definition	Measured Relation to Achievement Gains in Basic Skills Subjects
School Year	# days school in session	Small
Attendance Year	# days students present NOTE: # days teachers are not present is another important variable	Moderately Significant
Scheduled Time	Amount of time set aside for instruction in given content area	Moderately Significant
Allocated Time	Actual time devoted to instruction in given content area	Significant
Student Engaged Time	Actual amount of time during which students are actively involved in learning given content area	Significant
Academic Learning	Actual amount of time students are actively engaged in relevant learning activities at an appropriate level of success	Highly Significant

Allocated time is the amount of time designated or scheduled daily for a given subject area. Principals should require teachers to prepare a schedule of when and how long each subject is taught. At the high school level the schedule should include the number of periods each unit or topic will be taught. Prior to MBWA trips to classrooms the principal should determine the topic or subject in the schedule to be monitored. The MBWA visit offers the perfect opportunity to determine if the appropriate number of minutes are being devoted to the various subjects as planned.

Engaged time is the proportion of allocated time students spend actually working on a learning task or receiving instruction. The following work by Stallings (1984) shows the difference in engaged time between effective classrooms and those in which achievement falters.

ALLOCATED TIME FOR A FIFTY-MINUTE READING PERIOD

	Average Use	Effective Use
Off Task	12%	3%
Organizing	26%	12%
Active Instruction	12%	50%
Monitoring	50%	35%

Excellent classroom management is a prerequisite to achieving high rates of engaged time and is frequently the difference between the good and the marginal teacher. The first seven minutes are the key to classroom management. Wandering in about five minutes after the class is scheduled to start allows the principal to spend a minimum of two or three minutes and obtain maximum information. If instruction hasn't begun, a potential problem may exist. What the principal looks for is established routines, minimal confusion, and clearly communicated directions. Below are several indicators of effectively run classrooms that can be used to diagnose classroom management problems.

WHAT TO LOOK FOR

- Do the students know what to do?
- Are instructions written on the board?
- Are all materials readily available?
- Do students know what to do upon completing assignments?
- Is the climate orderly and business-like?
- Did instruction begin within seven minutes of the bell or transition?

The last five minutes are also an important time to gain insight into engaged time. Here the principal looks for the following:

- Does the period end with a clear explanation of homework expectations?
- Are students engaged in learning?
- Do students who finish early go on to the next task?

- Is the climate orderly and business-like?
- Is the teacher monitoring seat work?
- Is the transition to the next class smooth?

Success rate is the level of difficulty of the instructional task. The research is clear that new tasks should be at the 80 percent success level; that students should have the prerequisite knowledge and skills to correctly complete 80 percent of the tasks in each lesson. Students who are below that level experience frustration and struggle, often resulting in off task behavior. Students who are above that level are not challenged and, in fact, are having time wasted learning what they already know. A synthesis of the time on task research led Karwiet (1983) to conclude that success rate is more important to increasing achievement than engaged or allocated time. The point being that it's not a question of quantity—how much time students spend with their noses in a book. Instead, it's a question of quality. Is the task relevant and are students learning the material?

The first clue to task relevancy and success rate is whether or not the instructional objective is in the curriculum. Prior to visiting the class the principal should know what is supposed to be taught during that period. Once in the classroom there are two techniques for assessing success rate.

If children are working independently, ask them to read two paragraphs. If children make five or more errors, the reading level is too difficult. On non-reading tasks simply ask the pupil to explain what he or she is doing and whether it is difficult or easy. This is MBWA in its ultimate form.

In a teacher directed lesson, just count the number of correct responses given by students. Again, 80 percent of those who volunteer or are called on should respond correctly. Keeping a simple tally of correct and incorrect responses provides the needed data.

Finally, another excellent clue to look for is response opportunity—are all students given an opportunity to respond to questions? Using a simple seating chart like the one on page 79, a principal can code a plus (+) or minus (−) in the appropriate box and get an overview of both success rate and response opportunity. In the example below, sixteen questions were asked with fourteen correct responses for an 87 percent success rate. Notice, however, students seated in the rear or sides are not involved.

TEACHER'S DESK

++	−	+	+	
	++	++	+	
		+	+	
	+	−	+	
		+		

TWENTY NO-COST OPTIONS TO ENHANCE QUALITY TIME

Below are twenty no-cost ideas to improve the quality of instructional time. Being an instructional expert and leader, the MBWA principal has a myriad of "helpful options" to offer teachers. Knowledge of these options comes from experience, watching teaching, and the literature and can be used to enhance the quality of time devoted to any subject. These can be shared with teachers during MBWA visits, in conferences, or in faculty meetings where staff is asked to compare current practices with the suggested alternative or to create other alternatives. Time is our scarcest resource and must be spent wisely.

COMMON PRACTICE	QUALITY ALTERNATIVE
1. Show and tell—especially after 1st grade	**1.** Every Friday, teacher eats lunch in room—anyone who wants to tell teacher anything can eat in room with teacher
2. Writing all spelling words five or ten times	**2.** Give a pretest—write only words the child misses
3. Taking prime instructional time to make holiday decorations, practice plays, music, etc.	**3.** Have uninterrupted time for basic skill areas and that's all that's taught

COMMON PRACTICE	QUALITY ALTERNATIVE
4. Worksheets that don't relate to what has been taught	**4.** Worksheets must be provided on skills learned/taught
5. Free time (games, puzzles, etc.) during prime instructional time	**5.** If students finish, have them read or write in journal but not play a game unrelated to the objective
6. Any special holiday—time taken out of reading—not other, less critical areas	**6.** Scheduled activities are not taken out of reading time or have stipulation that reading will be taught sometime during the day
7. Excessive recess time in addition to normal P.E. time—often exceeds time given to science and math	**7.** Provide expected time per subject and monitor—require time schedule and lesson plan book
8. Too much time for spelling: 105 minutes a week—30 minutes a day	**8.** Seventy-five minutes per week is adequate for pupils in most grades—couple with reading groups rather than assign questionable worksheets
9. Movies—30 minutes a week	**9.** Probably not necessary
10. Parties—monthly birthdays, holidays, etc.	**10.** Allow so many parties per year—list acceptable parties as an expectation
11. Having P.E. "play days" 9 to 10:30 in the morning	**11.** Provide special, organized games different from P.E. routine
12. Visual clutter—this could distract students—perhaps not the teacher	**12.** Suggest appropriate use of walls and bulletin boards—see 15 below
13. Friday reward days—parties, movies, games, free time, record playing, dancing	**13.** Friday is like Monday—not a free day
14. Teacher teaching/speaking from seated position	**14.** All directed large-group instruction, unless the teacher is handicapped, is carried out from a standing position
15. Sloppy bulletin boards—no intent	**15.** Walls and bulletin boards are used to teach/illustrate concepts being studied or reinforce skills, i.e., countries studied, math facts, word lists, etc.

COMMON PRACTICE	QUALITY ALTERNATIVE
16. Book report forms required for books read; filling out a form for every book probably decreases attitudes toward reading rather than increasing desire to read more	**16.** Discussions about books or working with a partner to compare favorite characters
17. Students filling out a stack of worksheets for hours	**17.** Have more active participation, interaction, discussion with students
18. Students, one-by-one, reading percent scores from worksheets to teachers for posting in grade book	**18.** Teachers should do this or have an aide or friend post grades
19. Copying words, looking them up in the dictionary, and writing definitions	**19.** Vocabulary words need to be discussed and placed in context. Semantic mapping activities would be better
20. Science activities—building a volcano and related activities	**20.** This activity should be at another time during the school day, not during prime instructional time

AN ORDERLY ENVIRONMENT THROUGH EFFECTIVE DISCIPLINE

Discipline is the foundation of an effective school. After extensive study, the Philadelphia Public Schools Office of Research and Evaluation (Farber, 1979) concluded that good discipline impacted reading achievement more than did class size. Likewise, Edmonds (1982) cited it as one of his five correlates of an effective school. It is clear that learning does not take place without an orderly, productive climate. It is also clear that the principal bears the responsibility for discipline in the school.

Contrary to the old adage, discipline isn't the result of not smiling until Thanksgiving and long lists of don'ts. Discipline results from careful planning. The plan includes more than rules and consequences; it also embodies a thoughtful philosophy, a strategy for reinforcing students and staff for following the plan, and a means for communicating the plan to students, teachers, and parents.

A philosophy of discipline includes both the purpose and basic discipline models to be used. In a study of orderly schools Wayson et al. (1982) found that the purpose for discipline went well beyond just maintaining law and order.

COMMON AIMS OF WELL-DISCIPLINED SCHOOLS

(1) To improve the way in which people in school work together to solve problems

(2) To reduce authority and status differences among all persons in the school

(3) To develop rules and disciplinary procedures that will promote self-discipline

(4) To increase and widen students' sense of belonging in the school

(5) To improve curriculum and instructional practices in order to reach more students

(6) To deal with personal problems that affect life within the school

(7) To strengthen interaction between the school and home

(8) To improve the physical facilities and organizational structure of the school to reinforce the other goals

Everyone involved needs to understand the big picture, the rationale for the rules, the logic of the consequences, and how they relate to the overall philosophy of the discipline plan.

Incorporated in the plan should be a statement indicating the basic discipline models to be used and these should be congruent with the purposes. The one truism about discipline that seems to hold whether discussing parenting or classrooms is that consistency is the key. Given the broad array of models presented below, it is easy to see that the principal and staff need to reach agreement on how children will be disciplined.

The plan should also delineate the range of alternative consequences available as illustrated by Wolfgang and Glickman (1980) in Figure 5.1. There are great differences between a student disrupting class by arriving late or talking out of turn as opposed to cussing out the teacher or having an extreme tantrum. Teachers need to know before the incident what options are available in dealing with hard-core problems. The continuum in Figure 5.2 is illustrative of such a continuum of alternatives.

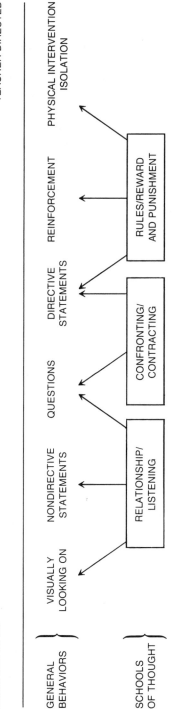

CHILD CENTERED

TEACHER DIRECTED

GENERAL BEHAVIORS: VISUALLY LOOKING ON, NONDIRECTIVE STATEMENTS, QUESTIONS, DIRECTIVE STATEMENTS, REINFORCEMENT, PHYSICAL INTERVENTION ISOLATION

SCHOOLS OF THOUGHT: RELATIONSHIP/LISTENING, CONFRONTING/CONTRACTING, RULES/REWARD AND PUNISHMENT

MODELS: TEACHER EFFECTIVENESS TRAINING, TRANSACTIONAL ANALYSIS, VALUE CLARIFICATION, DISCIPLINE WITHOUT TEARS, REALITY THERAPY, BEHAVIOR MODIFICATION, DARE TO DISCIPLINE, ASSERTIVE DISCIPLINE

FIGURE 5.1 Teacher behavior continuum. Reprinted with permission from Wolfgang, C. H. and C. S. Glickman. *Solving Discipline Problems: Strategies for Classroom Teachers*. Boston:Allyn & Bacon (1980).

No matter how detailed or well-publicized, the plan will falter if the principal does not get into classrooms to encourage, support, and reinforce teachers implementing the program (see Figure 5.2). The week before school starts, the principal needs to meet individually with teachers to see that rules and procedures are ready. There should be no more than five classroom rules and they should be posted in the room. Procedures should include how routine daily chores will be handled, how lessons will begin and end, and what students are to do when in need of help or when finished with seat work. The principal also scans classroom physical environments to ensure that teachers can observe all students and move easily around the room. Finally, teachers need a plan and schedule as to how they will instruct the students about the rules and procedures. Sample policies and plans can be found in Appendices G and H.

The time invested in the first week is critical. In research conducted on effective classroom management, the effective teachers were found: (1) to spend a maximum amount of time with pupils explaining rules and procedures clearly, with examples and reasons; (2) to actually teach children the appropriate behavior, such as lining up, responding to signals, etc.; (3) to use a variety of positive reinforcers; and (4) to constantly monitor behavior and respond promptly to misbehavior.

Finally, teachers need a plan for how the principal will be involved in discipline. It needs to be clear under what circumstances students will be sent to the office, and it must be clear what consequence or action will be taken by the principal. If the teacher views the consequence as too harsh or too lenient, it will undermine the discipline plan. There should be no surprises as to how the student is dealt with and the outcome of the discipline referral.

The checklist below is provided as a guide for principals to assist teachers in planning for an orderly classroom.

EFFECTIVE CLASSROOM MANAGEMENT GUIDE

1. Has clearly defined procedures and routines ready for the first day of school □ Yes   □ No
  - how daily chores will be done
  - how lessons will begin and end
  - what to do when a student is finished or needs help
  - clearly communicates rules and consequences

MINOR DISCIPLINE ———————————————————————————————————— MAJOR DISCIPLINE

CLASSROOM GUIDANCE TECHNIQUES	SHORTENED DAY	RESOURCE PROGRAM	SELF-CONTAINED E. H. PROGRAM
BEHAVIORAL MANAGEMENT	IN HOUSE SUPERVISION	COUNSELING	*
STUDY SKILLS	TIME OUT	LONG-TERM SUSPENSION	*
LOSS OF PRIVILEGES	SHORT-TERM SUSPENSION	*	*
REWARDS	COUNSELING	*	*
DEMERITS	PARENT EDUCATION	*	EXPULSION
*	PERSONAL ADVOCATES	*	
*	SYSTEMATIC SUSPENSION		
*	*		
	MEDIATION		
	*		

FIGURE 5.2 Continuum of discipline alternatives.

2. Teaches the procedures and routines as instructional content
☐ Yes   ☐ No

3. Monitors behavior ☐ Yes   ☐ No
  • consistently scans the room
  • doesn't remain stationary
  • practices prevention as opposed to reacting to problems

4. Handles inappropriate behavior promptly and consistently
☐ Yes   ☐ No
  • uses eye contact and proximity control
  • reminds pupil of the rule
  • asks student to repeat the rule
  • directs student to stop inappropriate behavior

5. Plans ahead ☐ Yes   ☐ No
  • has well-planned lessons
  • provides variety and challenge in seat work
  • has a contingency plan ready for emergency such as rainy
    weather

6. Utilizes supplemental management techniques to help non-conforming
students ☐ Yes   ☐ No

The long-run solution to discipline rests in teaching children
how to resolve problems peacefully and begin to assume personal
responsibility for school discipline (Clewett, 1988 and Brandt,
1988). The Conflict Managers Program developed in the San
Francisco Public Schools is such a program. Students are taught
basic mediation skills such as active listening and clarifying, and
once trained they are adorned in bright easily recognizable T-
shirts and sent to patrol the play areas. Children learn to seek
out a conflict manager to mediate a dispute rather than fighting.

The long-range goals of all discipline is to teach children
socially acceptable ways to resolve problems. This calls for a well
thought-out and effectively implemented plan. Such plans cannot
be decreed from on high. The MBWA leader works with teachers
to develop it, provides resources needed to implement it, is out
and about on the campus and in classrooms to see how it is working, and helps where possible.

MBWA IN THE COMMUNITY

Another major finding of the effective schools research is that of
involving parents in activities related directly to improving stu-

dent performance (Robinson, 1985). Why? Involved parents develop an ownership in the school's mission, and the ownership breeds cooperation. The same is true for the non-school-age parents in your school area or school district. Schools exist to serve the community. The community, at least in part, pays the bills and sends its young people to us. Schools need community support in order to achieve their missions for students. What role does MBWA play in the community?

Take advantage of every opportunity (such as PTA meetings, concerts, athletic events, open houses, award programs and non-school events such as carnivals, picnics, and church events) to mix with parents and other community members. First, you must attend as many of these functions as practicable. If you are not available, send a designee. Before and after each event take time to mingle. Wear a name tag and introduce yourself to as many people as you can without seeming as though you are campaigning for political office. Taking time to chat about their children can further develop the trust and respect aspects of the relationship. Communicate your concerns and expectations for the students and the school. Let them know you have their youngster's interest at heart.

There are great opportunities to practice preventative firefighting, sometimes called "rumor control." If a rumor is loose, share the truth so that people are equipped to deal with it in a healthy way. Rumors are sometimes spread by some people simply because they do not know what else to believe. Arm them with facts and they can act as rumor exterminators.

Keep in contact with your community, extend your hand when you meet and greet them, make them feel welcome, be warm, put your ingratiation skills to use, let them know how great your school is and what it needs to be even better, show your interest and concern for their children, and involve them in a very active and responsible way in important projects. Last but not least, listen very closely to what they say. Don't think of what you will say when they finish speaking, just listen!

Keeping the community informed, involving them in school activities, getting the good word out about your school, organizing them to help solve the school problems, starting school programs, and conducting effective rumor control are more than one principal can accomplish and are beyond the scope of ordinary MBWA-ing. Good news, you don't have to do it all yourself and no one expects you to. But you are *responsible* for seeing that these activities take place. Expanded MBWA is the answer! Empower other people; put them to work and give them responsibility.

As alluded to before, no one "human" principal can meet, touch, and inform all the members of a school or school district community. There are simply not enough hours in a year. The goals are to:

(1) Provide accurate information to members of your community regarding good things happening in your school or district.
(2) Correct misinformation through rumor control.
(3) Build strong pride, ownership, and partnership in the school.
(4) Provide members with a thorough and accurate understanding of the school's needs to gain support for fund raising, bond issues, and other public votes regarding school finances.

Two effective programs for accomplishing all of these activities with the community by expanding your MBWA capacity are described below.

PLAN 1: KEY COMMUNICATORS

Concept: Develop a team of twenty to thirty parents and non-parents including retired people with the goal of informing them of the good things going on in the school and the challenges being faced by the school. This group will serve as "key communicators" in the community and their job is to keep others informed, stamp out rumors with accurate information, and develop the invaluable and equally intangible feelings of pride and partnership in the community.

So how do you organize such a group? Here are the steps.

(1) Develop the idea, purposes, timelines, and activities in your head. Then cover the bases at central office. If you are a superintendent, cover the "board" bases. Our experience tells us that you should not ask for permission. Instead share the benefits and the idea of what you are going to do and ask for suggestions to make it better. There's a big difference. The former opens the door to say "no." The latter gives them the opportunity to put *their mark* on a great idea.

(2) Detail the purpose of the meeting. It is likely to be information dissemination and maybe some group work to get the key communicators actively involved. Use the forms provided in Chapter VII for this step.

(3) Select an appropriate meeting place and take care of details: proper seating, name tags, refreshments, visuals, etc. Follow the guidelines in Chapter VII for hints on setting up for meetings.

Order large notebooks with the names of your school and KEY COMMUNICATORS printed on the front. This will be the communicators' tool for organizing the information you give to them at the meeting. They can carry this with them to neighborhood meetings for easy reference. This is listed as KEY COMMUNICATOR ORGANIZATIONAL MATERIALS in the sample agenda on page 90.

(4) Develop the agenda. What topics do you want to address? First, let them know the purpose of the key communicator group and why they are there. Be sure to include recent accomplishments and "how" they happened. You and your staff probably worked hard to accomplish these. Let them know about it. Give credit to all those involved: students, parents, teachers, local business, etc. Give credit to yourself too but low-key it. They know you're responsible; modesty and humility pay big dividends in terms of their respect and esteem for you as the "leader."

Use the guidelines in Chapter VII for planning the agenda. Sample agenda topics for an initial key communicator meeting are provided on the following page.

(5) Advertise the formation of the key communicator group and its purpose in the local paper, the school newsletter, and district newsletter. A sample press release is provided on page 90. Note the purposes outlined in the article and the open invitation to join. Include key information such as who, what, when, why, and where in your press release.

(6) Who will attend? It is easy to invite just those who have been friendly in the past, but don't take the easy way out. Invite some critics! You have a good school; help them know just how good it is and how they can help make it better by being a partner. When they become active in a participating partnership effort, they are likely to become staunch supporters.

KEY COMMUNICATOR INFORMATION MEETING:
SAMPLE AGENDA

   I. Introductions
  II. Purpose of key communicator program
 III. Key communicator organizational materials
 IV. School (district) information
     A. Enrollment growth—projections
     B. Construction projects
     C. Boundary line changes
     D. Transportation committee
     E. Student Achievements
       1. Athletics
       2. Test scores
       3. Academics and fine arts
     F. New programs
     G. Parent survey results
     H. Compensation program
  V. Questions and answers
 VI. Time and date of next meeting

SAMPLE PRESS RELEASE

The Canyon View School is initiating a new program to increase public awareness of school events and programs.

About twenty volunteers from the Canyon View community will participate in the key communicator program by holding and/or participating in meetings throughout the community to inform community members of the school's achievements and challenges.

"We are finding that many members of the community are very interested in education but are unaware of all the outstanding programs that exist in our school. We want to help them learn of these," Chris Ahearn, Principal of Canyon View, said.

"So we decided to do something about that. The volunteers will meet with me once a month to learn of Canyon View 'happenings,' then go out to their neighborhoods and hold meetings to let others know about CVSD. They will become the neighborhood experts. In addition to me and the PTA members, people will be able to ask questions of them. We are hoping parents, grandparents, retirees, and business leaders will volunteer."

Parents and non-parents in the Canyon View community interested in becoming a key communicator can contact Ahearn by calling 666-7777. The first meeting will be held in the Canyon View School Library at 7:00 PM, Wednesday, January 15, 1988.

They need a feeling of responsibility for what's going on. Empower them, share some of your power, give them some responsibility, give them some room to create, and give them room to "try out" ideas and reap the rewards. Those who are empowered are strong workers and their creative abilities and desires to participate are unleashed. Those who are locked out become bitter enemies.

Stakeholders and movers and shakers from all groups (parents representing all grade levels, grandparents, retirees, business leaders, and representatives from interest groups) should be included.

(7) Invite the press by letter and a follow-up call. Include the agenda for the meeting to whet their appetites. Give them a sample press release for use the day following the meeting. Build up the key communicator concept. Make inclusion of your idea in their newspaper easy.

(8) Send follow-up invitations to those who have volunteered to attend and those you selected. Stress the importance of the key communicator program and their role in it. Give them strong reason to feel important and welcome. A sample letter is shown on page 92.

(9) Conduct the meeting.

(10) Send out thank you letters and include information on the next meeting date and any activities agreed to at the meeting.

(11) Send copies of all of this to your supervisors. They will love it.

(12) Send follow-up letters to the press and include an article in the district and school newsletters about the program.

PLAN 2: PUBLIC INFORMATION SPECIALISTS

Concept: Assemble and train a cadre of teachers and/or community members to conduct public information dissemination activities for your school/district.

Steps for developing this group follow.

(1) Advertise for the position(s). We suggest one per elementary school with enrollment of 700 students or less and one additional position for each additional 1500 students. Include the

SAMPLE INVITATION LETTER

Dear Mr. Smith:

The first meeting of the CANYON VIEW SCHOOL KEY COMMUNI-
CATORS has been scheduled for Wednesday, January 15, 1988, at
7:00 P.M. in the Canyon View library.

Topics to be addressed at this meeting include the following:

PURPOSE OF KEY COMMUNICATORS
ENROLLMENT GROWTH
NEW SCHOOL BOUNDARIES
NEW PROGRAMS
STUDENT ACHIEVEMENTS
QUESTIONS AND ANSWERS
NEXT MEETING

I sincerely hope that you will attend this meeting. The KEY COMMU-
NICATORS will play a very valuable role in the growth and improvement of our school. You can certainly be a very valuable asset in
this effort.

I look forward to seeing you on the 15th.

Sincerely,

Chris Ahearn
Principal

purpose of the position in the advertisement—"to inform,
through the news media, the Sunrise Drive School and Tucson Communities of the many great education programs and
people in our community through an active public information program." Duties include setting up systems for gathering information on Sunrise Drive happenings, writing press
releases, and communicating with newspaper editors, TV and
radio managers, and Key Communicators, and select public
officials and politicians. A sample job description is provided
on page 93.

(2) Who are the candidates? Teachers, parents, or other adult community members may apply. Highly mature and qualified high school students are also a possibility in select cases. Key qualifications include ability to organize systems, verbal and written communication skills, availability of time, and desire to serve the school. Familiarity with members of the media is also very important. The authors have found that both parents and teachers can do a great job in these positions.

(3) Training is crucial. Hire a professional PR expert or recruit the PR expert from your central office to train your team. Training should include skills for writing press releases; techniques for gaining an audience with the media; how to scoop out and select hot story topics; how to develop and organize files of media names, addresses, and phone numbers; determining best times for submitting press releases; and how to conduct follow-up.

(4) Set objectives for the school year. "Providing media coverage" is too general! The more specific the objectives, the more likely they will be realized. Examples of specific goals are shown at the top of page 94.

PUBLIC INFORMATION SPECIALIST
JOB DESCRIPTION

Objective: Further enhance public awareness of the many fine activities taking place in the Sunrise Drive School

Stipend: $1,000 per year

Duties: 1. Prepare and distribute press releases for newsworthy events taking place at the Sunrise Drive School.
2. Insure presence of news reporters at school events.
3. Present press releases of the three most newsworthy activities taking place each month at the school to the district and school newsletter writers.
4. Prepare announcements and invitations to school activities and present to local businesses and organizations for distribution.
5. Other related duties as assigned by the administration.

GOALS FOR SY 88–89

—To publish four feature stories with area newspapers.

Each representative will develop one feature centered around a basic theme. One story will be published each quarter. The four themes are Crisis Management, Human Relations, Arts in the School, and Being a Good Neighbor.

—To publish Canyon View events and awards in the local media.

Each representative will be responsible for keeping the media informed of their school's calendar of special events and/or awards of recognition received.

—To assist in the development of a comprehensive public relations plan for the district.

Each representative will participate on the Comprehensive Public Relations Plan Task Force.

In this plan, each school's Public Information Specialist works in tandem with the district PR program. The advantages are obvious but the school can run its program independently of the districts if desired. This is crucial in cases where the district does not have an organized PR program. Just wait, when they see the benefits of your program, they will implement one posthaste.

The purpose of these programs is to expand your MBWA capabilities by empowering those around you to share the responsibility. You can wander forever and not get the job done. The school needs you as a leader to organize the entire team to accomplish the school's mission. Great leaders are great organizers of human talent. Good leaders are always interested in new and successful ideas. Good luck. Please share your experiences with us.

SAFE AND ORDERLY PHYSICAL ENVIRONMENT

The effective schools research has identified a "safe and orderly environment," including the physical facility and discipline, as one of the key characteristics of an effective school. Sounds incredibly obvious, doesn't it? Well, it is, but how many schools do not possess these characteristics? We know their numbers are legion. This is a good place to start with MBWA.

PHYSICAL FACILITIES

The effective schools research found a sense of quiet pride in high-achieving schools and a sense of caring that was reflected in the positive physical appearance of a school where repairs are made immediately (Robinson, 1985, p. 18). As one successful principal said, "I want to set a tone that permeates the environment. I want my actions to speak. If you keep the floors and walls nice, it's like having your shoes shined and a clean shirt on" (Peters and Austin, 1984, p. 399). Walk through a clean school, a school that is nicely decorated with the mission of the school and student work, a school that is well-maintained with fresh paint, clean windows, and an obvious absence of dirt and litter and you feel pride. It's an inviting place. It has the same impact on the teachers, students, staff, and parents who visit. It helps communicate the mission of the school, the ownership, and the pride; it grows on all those involved. People like being there, and they will be back to join the team effort in accomplishing things *for* the school and its students. A story about Mr. Ray Kroc, owner of a McDonald's chain, communicates one man's vision and "quiet pride":

> One day while on his way back to the office from an important lunch at the best restaurant in town, he asked his driver to pass through a few McDonald's parking lots. In one parking lot he spotted papers caught up in the wind screen of shrubs along the outer fence. He immediately went to the nearest pay phone, called his office to get the name of the manager, then called the manager to offer to help him pick up the trash in the parking lot. Both the owner of the McDonald's chain, Ray Kroc, in his expensive business suit and the young manager met in the parking lot and got on their hands and knees to pick up the paper.

As educational administrators we are frequently more interested in instruction and educational programs than the appearance of the school. The "look" of the school is your first line of PR with the community. Show them a well-kept facility and they are likely to be supportive. Show them an unkempt, dirty, and abused facility and they may refuse to spend more tax dollars for facilities when the buildings funded by the last bond issue are not taken care of. As with any other investment, they want evidence that their investment in the school is healthy and not deteriorating.

Deteriorating or unclean facilities will catch up to you and bite you right where it stings. This can and has happened to the best of administrators. The authors recall a perfect illustration. This principal was a model instructional leader. He could demonstrate instructional techniques, provide insightful critiques of his teachers' lessons, give practical and valid recommendations for improvement, move the forces at central office to acquire the materials and equipment his teachers needed, and handle discipline problems with ease. He did it all, except pay attention to what his school looked like. As we visited the school, it became obvious to us that the instructional program was top notch but the facility was "the pits." Paper and milk cartons littered the grounds, paint was pealing off the metal supports, classroom ceilings were covered with water stains, sidewalks were serving as absorption pads for sour milk, water fountains leaked or did not work, shingles were missing from the roof, many pieces of playground equipment were broken, and the windows were dirty. Parents and teachers began recognizing this sad state of affairs too and began their political push for improvements. As practitioners know, parents are not always gentle. In this case the administration was bloodied a bit. It took a year to get the school back in shape and the principal learned a big lesson; all were a bit wiser. Now observation of the facility is an important part of the principal's MBWA schedule and communicates his "quiet pride."

The instructional program may be excellent and deserve that "quiet pride," but an unsafe, unpleasant, unkept, and unclean environment is noticed first and will overshadow the program's excellence. Eventually it will lead to mistrust and words and actions of anger.

So, what specifically do you look for regarding the physical plant when you are wandering around? A handy checklist follows. Readers are also referred to Lober (1988) for a helpful guide to facilities maintenance.

Facilities Checklist

Grounds

shrubbery–trimmed, adequate in number, healthy

sidewalks–clean, in good repair

parking areas–well-marked, adequate size, in good repair, adequate lighting, paint–peeling, faded

drainage–accommodates volume demand, in good repair, clear of debris, grass–watered, fertilized, level, recently mowed, worn areas

fencing–in good repair, damaged, painted or maintained as needed, adequate to meet the demands, posts in good order, retaining walls–painted or otherwise treated, cracks

Exterior of buildings

walls–painted or otherwise treated as prescribed, plumb, settlement cracks, waterproof

roof–blisters, seams, cracked riders, coping, other evidence of leaks, missing shingles, visually attractive, gutters and downspouts–firmly secured, free of debris, well-maintained

openings/windows–caulking, cracking, weatherstripping, screens

openings/doors–condition of paint, condition of doors, weatherstripping, checks, holders, kick plates, thresholds

fire escapes–condition of paint, structural integrity, working order

lighting–working, covers in good order

Interior of buildings

walls–painted, holes repaired, no grafitti

stairs–treads, handrails, lighting

floors–floor mats, baseboards, clean, maintained

lockers–good condition

trim–good condition

drinking fountains–adequate number, working order, clean

Sanitary facilities

toilets–ventilation, cleanliness, lighting, adequate number

fixtures—urinals, stools, tissue holders, towel holders in working order and clean

Ventilation

heating—working order, regular maintenance
cooling—same as above

The list seems endless and it can be, especially if you do not ensure that all are in good order. A few hours each month will save many headaches and many more hours down the road. Facilities do not have to be new, but there is no excuse for them to be dirty. A clean well-kept campus helps instill a sense of pride in both the students and the community. We suggest assigning these monitoring functions to the head custodian. MBWA is for everyone, not just the principal, and in light of the demands on your time this is a perfect opportunity to delegate and practice time management.

These items must be inspected anywhere from twice a year (roofs) to once each week (toilet rooms) and needed action taken. Emergencies should be reported to you immediately, and a full report regarding the facilities should be provided to you at least one month in advance of the central office deadline for submitting capital budget requests.

Final note—some of the items in the list seem trivial? They sure do, but the most trivial can deliver the nastiest sting. In the situation described above, the door stops were missing from the doors, and during the warmer months the doors were held open with rocks. Seems pretty reasonable—rocks can certainly do the job. Well, it seemed reasonable until the health and safety inspector paid a visit. The absence of door stops and the use of a rock was duly noted and included in the report which was delivered directly to the board president, shared with other board members and eventually the parents. The information made the gossip-loop and became exaggerated—"we can't afford doors or door stops," "the children are in immediate danger," and "the administrator doesn't care about the welfare of children." Of course, none of the above was true, but a person's perception is his reality. Changing realities such as these takes a lot of time. Time you don't have. So start your MBWA in regard to the safety of the environment now!

REFERENCES

ANDERSON, L. M., C. M. Evertson and J. E. Brophy. "An Experimental Study of Effective Teaching in First-Grade Teaching Groups," *The Elementary School Journal*, 79:193–223 EJ 201 788 (1979).

BARTON, S. and L. Morrison. "Getting Off to a Good Start with Discipline," *Teach. Educ.* 23:30–32 (Spring 1988).

BRANDT, R. "Our Student's Needs and Team Learning: A Conversation with William Glasser," *Educational Leadership,* 45:38–45 (March 1988).

BROWN, W. E. and L. T. Payne. "Discipline In-Service Training in the Public Schools: Teacher Responses and a Proposed Model," *Education.* 108:511–515 (Summer 1988).

CARTER, M. "Effective School Discipline Through Democratic Participation," *Phi Delta Kappan.* Bloomington:IN (May 1987).

CHAMBERLIN, L. and J. Sommerville. "Improving the Discipline Techniques of Beginning Teachers," *Am. Second. Educ.* 16(4):28–30 (1988).

CLEWETT, A. S. "Discipline as Teaching Rather Than Punishment," *The Education Digest*, 54:40–43 (November 1988).

CUNNINGHAM, B. and A. Sugawara. "Preservice Teachers' Perceptions of Children's Problem Behaviors," *Jour. Educ. Res.* 82:34–39 (S/O 1988).

DEROUCHE, E. F. *An Administrator's Guide for Evaluating Programs and Personnel: An Effective Schools Approach,* 2nd edition. Massachusetts:Allyn and Bacon (1988).

EDMONDS, R. "Programs of School Improvement: An Overview," *Educational Leadership*, 40:4–11 (December 1982).

"Effectively Disciplined Schools" (Symposium). *NASSP Bull.*, 72:1–6+ (January 1988).

ERICKSON, H. L. "The Boy Who Couldn't Be Disciplined," *Principal*, 67:36–37 (May 1988).

EMMER, E. T., C. M. Evertson, and L. M. Anderson. "Effective Classroom Management at the Beginning of the School Year," *Elementary School Journal,* 80(5):219–231 (1980).

"Evaluation of Administrators" (Symposium). *NASSP Bull.* 72:1–6+ (May 1988).

FARBER, I., M. H. Kean, M. J. Vaivetz, and A. A. Sunmers. *What Works in Reading?* Philadelphia:Office of Research and Evaluation, The School District of Philadelphia (1979).

FELDMAN, P. R. E. B. "Good Maintenance Is Good," *Am. Sch. Univ.* 60:36+ (April 1988).

GOOTMAN, M. "Discipline Alternatives That Work," *The Humanist,* 48:11–13+ (1988).

GOUGH, P. B. "The Key to Improving Schools: An Interview with William Glasser," *Phi Delta Kappan.* 68:656–662 (May 1987).

JOHNSON, K. "Handling the Tough Ones: Crisis Management with Children," *Thrust*, 17:31–33 (January 1988).

HATHAWAY, W. E. "Light, Colour & Air Quality: Important Elements of the Learning Environment?" *Educ. Can.,* 27:35–44 (Fall 1987); *Discussion*, 28:45–47 (Fall 1988).

KARWIET, N. L. *Time on Task: A Research Review.* Baltimore, MD:The Johns Hopkins Univ. Center for Solid Organization of Schools (1983).

LASLEY, T. S. and W. Wayson. "Characteristics of Schools with Good Discipline," *Educational Leadership,* pp. 28–31 (December 1982).

LOBER, I. *School Facilities Maintenance and Operations Manual.* Reston, VA:Association of School Business Officials International (1988).

MAJOR, R. L. "Discipline and the First Year Teacher," *Clearing House.* 61:221–222 (January 1988).

McCURDY, B. L. and E. S. Shapiro. "Self-Observation and the Reduction of Inappropriate Classroom Behavior," *Jour. Sch. Psychol.* 26:371–378 (Winter 1988).

NIECE, R. "Facility Planning and Curriculum Design–The Impact of Environment on Teaching and Learning," *NASSP Bull.,* 72:79–81 (May 1988).

NIGHSWANDER, J. K. *School Discipline–A Planning and Resource Guide.* Wheeling, IL:National School Services (1987).

ORTON, R. L. "Start a P.M. Program," *Am. Sch. Univ.,* 60:48d (April 1988).

PETERS, T. and N. Austin. *A Passion for Excellence: The Leadership Difference.* New York:Random House (1984).

PICCIGALLO, P. R. "Renovating Urban Schools Is Fundamental to Improving Them," *Phi Delta Kappan,* 70:402–406 (January 1989).

REECER, M. "When Students Say School Makes Them Sick, Sometimes They're Right," *Am. Sch. Board Jour.,* 176:16–21 (August 1988).

ROBINSON, G. "Effective Schools Research: Guide to School Improvement," *Concerns in Education Series.* Educational Research Service, Inc. (Feb. 1985).

ROGERS, D. *Classroom Discipline: An Idea Handbook for Elementary School Teachers,* 2nd edition. Englewood Cliffs, NJ:Prentice-Hall (1987).

STALLINGS, J. *Effective Use of Class Time.* Charleston, West Virginia:Appalachia Educational Laboratory, p. 14 (1984).

STEWART, G. K. and D. S. Honeyman. "Capital Outlay and Deferred Maintenance in Kansas," *Jour. Educ. Finance,* 13:7–23 (Winter 1988).

WALSH, J. A. *Timekeeping in the Classroom.* Charleston, West Virginia:Appalachia Educational Laboratory, p. 5 (Nov. 1985).

WAYSON, W. W. *Handbook for Developing Schools with Good Discipline.* Bloomington, IN:Phi Delta Kappa (1982).

WHELDALL, K. and F. M. S. Bayless. "Why the Loudest Lads Are Most Likely to Succeed of Which Classroom Behaviors Do Primary Schoolteachers Say They Find Most Troublesome?" *Times Educ. Suppl.,* 3765:7 (August 26, 1988).

WOLFGANG, C. H. and C. S. Glickman. *Solving Discipline Problems: Strategies for Classroom Teachers.* Boston:Allyn & Bacon (1980).

CHAPTER
VI

Dealing with Unmet Expectations:
The Marginal Teacher

THE purpose of supervision and professional development programs is to assist teachers in doing their job effectively. Teachers come into the profession to help young people learn, and it is the administrator's job to help them succeed. Chapter V dealt with developing and implementing professional development programs to keep top-quality teachers on the cutting edge and help others get there. Helping teachers do their best for students is a very noble venture; it's like motherhood, apple pie, and Porsches. Who could object? The not so pleasant side of professional development is that not all teachers attain minimum standards regardless of how much help is given.

There is reason to believe that many students in the public schools are not receiving the quality of teaching they deserve. The reason is incompetent teachers. Some experts estimate that 5% to 15% of practicing teachers are either incompetent or below reasonable standards (Johnson, 1984, Neill and Custis, 1978). Assuming that even the more conservative estimate of 5% is accurate, the actual number of incompetent teachers in our schools is a whopping 110,000, enough to staff every classroom in the 14 smallest states (Bridges, 1985, p. 2). Assuming that these incompetent teachers instruct classes of 18.9 students each (Bridges, 1985, p. 16), the future of 2.7 million students is jeopardized each year. The severity of the problem can no longer be in doubt, and educators can no longer ignore it.

A reasonable question at this time is "what does MBWA have to do with teacher dismissal?" The answer is clear and simple — the MBWA principal makes frequent classroom walk-throughs and

101

teacher observations. That's the only way he can be intimately familiar with each teacher's strengths and weaknesses. The problem is that such visits are a rarity. As shown in Chapter VII, on the average, principals spend only 2.5 to 10% of their time in classrooms. This minuscule amount of time spent in classrooms is reflected in principals' evaluations of teachers. A recent review of principals' rating of teachers revealed that principals rank 98.2% of the teachers as perfect and only two-tenths of 1 percent as unsatisfactory (Langlois and Colarusso, 1988). Both of these figures fall far short of the well calculated estimates reported above. Inflated scores such as these destroy school administrators' credibility, both from their teachers and the public they serve. As will be seen in the following pages, detecting and taking the necessary action to eliminate incompetency takes time and requires principals to be in classrooms 50+% of their time.

Dealing with teachers who do not meet expectations is what this chapter is all about.

ANALYZING TEACHER PERFORMANCE

Strong supervision and evaluation programs identify top-notch teachers, capable teachers, teachers of marginal ability, and incompetents. George Ordiorne (1983), who popularized management by objectives, offers the following model for conceptualizing teacher performance classifications. The two dimensions used are *performance* and *potential* of the individual (see Figure 6.1).

The WORKHORSE is the overachieving teacher whose performance is high but potential is low to moderate. This teacher comes to work every day and gives 100 percent and keeps the school going. Approximately 40–45 percent of all teachers fall in this category.

The STAR is the Jimmy Brown or the Bernie Kosar of teaching. These teachers do it all and very well. They make administrators look good; parents love them and students love them. They do a *great* job for the students and the school. This is a relatively small group, though, approximately 5–10 percent of all teachers.

The DEADWOOD is just that. Teachers in this category possess the same potential as the workhorses but lack the drive and motivation to perform. They do not respond to help, advice, or en-

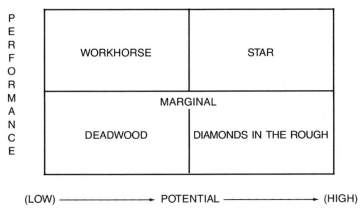

FIGURE 6.1 Employee-performance-analysis model.

couragement. They stay in teaching for their own reasons and tend to drag others down to their level. Deadwood accounts for approximately 5–10 percent of teachers.

The DIAMONDS IN THE ROUGH have high potential but are short on performance. New teachers are in this category. Polishing with professional development will hopefully put them into the STAR or WORKHORSE categories; 20–25 percent of the teachers fall into this classification.

The MARGINAL teacher is consistently low in performance, and has low to moderate potential; 10–20 percent of all teachers are in this category.

No profession wants or condones the presence of deadwood or marginal employees. The question becomes what to do with them. The first action step is to extend a helping hand through professional development, counseling, or whatever other measure is appropriate. The school district should help its teachers for at least two reasons. The first reason is one of economy. The district should follow through with its original investment of hiring and training them. The second reflects a moral obligation. The teachers come to the district in good faith to do a good job, and the district has an obligation to help the teachers succeed. Helping teachers improve reflects a basic value of a civilized and compassionate society, and that's what professional development is all about–helping teachers acquire the skills they need to succeed (see Chapter IV).

"How much obligation and for how long?" becomes very important to the school principal. There is no clear-cut answer; it will vary for each teacher in question. In the past and to a large extent today, very few, if any, teachers were ever dismissed because of inadequate performance in the classroom. Those whose abilities were recognized as inadequate were kept on the payroll because they were "nice," were believed to be "trying hard," were good football coaches, or possessed some other quality unrelated to their main job, classroom teaching. In these cases administrators were subject to the "savior syndrome"; they believed they could make a difference where previous administrators failed. They believed that *every* teacher possessed the potential and desire to do well. The reality is that approximately 10 percent of employees in industry whose performance is not adequate ever attain a rating of adequate or higher (Pfeiffer, 1984). This percentage matches the author's experience in public schools.

Although it appears morally right, adopting the savior syndrome is wrong. First, it is not morally right. The administrator's first responsibility is to ensure that only competent teachers are in contact with students, not protect those who cannot do the job. Schools were never intended to be havens or halfway houses for inadequate teachers. Second, if the 10 percent success rate is accurate, and the author believes it is, spending inordinate amounts of time on those who are not likely to improve, as demonstrated by past performance and attitude, is a gross misuse of precious district resources. This is another illustration of Pariato's law: 20 percent of the people create 80 percent of the problems and consume 80 percent of the resources. What about the other 80 percent of the people, the workhorses, the stars, and the new teachers who will bring success to education? They should get their fair share of the resources.

FORMS OF INCOMPETENCE

Bridges (1985)[b] has identified the following five forms of incompetence.

TECHNICAL—is deficient in one or more of the following: discipline, teaching methods, knowledge of subject matter, explanation of concepts, evaluation of pupil performance, organization, planning, etc.

BUREAUCRATIC—does not comply with school rules and regulations or directives of supervisors. Examples are failure to follow suggestions for improving performance, the district curriculum, or to allow supervisors in the classroom for purposes of observing performance.

ETHICAL—does not conform to standards of conduct applicable to the teaching profession. Examples are physical or psychological abuse of students, negative attitudes toward students, and indifference toward performance of teaching duties.

PRODUCTIVE—fails to obtain certain desirable results in the classroom, e.g., academic progress of students, interests of students toward school, respect of students for teacher, classroom climate, etc.

PERSONAL FAILURE—lacks certain emotional or physical attributes deemed instrumental in teaching. Poor judgement, emotional instability, lack of self-control and insufficient strength to withstand the rigors of teaching.

DEALING WITH MARGINAL TEACHERS

Dismissing inadequate teachers is not easy. It takes intestinal fortitude, time, and energy. A comprehensive process (adapted from Redfern, 1983) for dealing with a teacher from the time problems are first detected through dismissal is provided and discussed below.

1.1—The following process is an administrative guide for dealing with performance problems from time of initial detection of deficiencies through termination of services, when warranted. Termination is obviously very serious and strictly governed by law. Not everyone has the ability to teach, but that assumption/decision cannot be applied to an individual until due process has been followed. Due process can be a pain, but it is important. It is a compassionate society's attempt to ensure that those being dismissed are protected from arbitrary prejudices, vendettas, and other unethical motives for termination of employment. Due process may appear to provide unjust protection, but it is the best system available and must be followed scrupulously. Principals who follow due process to the letter are much more likely to have their decision upheld while those who fight due process are likely to lose on technical or ethical counts. For a detailed discussion of

A FOUR-PHASE PROCESS FOR DEALING
WITH THE MARGINAL TEACHER

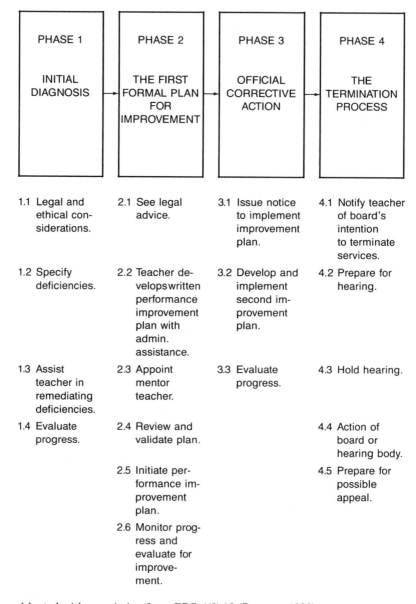

PHASE 1	PHASE 2	PHASE 3	PHASE 4
INITIAL DIAGNOSIS	THE FIRST FORMAL PLAN FOR IMPROVEMENT	OFFICIAL CORRECTIVE ACTION	THE TERMINATION PROCESS
1.1 Legal and ethical considerations.	2.1 See legal advice.	3.1 Issue notice to implement improvement plan.	4.1 Notify teacher of board's intention to terminate services.
1.2 Specify deficiencies.	2.2 Teacher develops written performance improvement plan with admin. assistance.	3.2 Develop and implement second improvement plan.	4.2 Prepare for hearing.
1.3 Assist teacher in remediating deficiencies.	2.3 Appoint mentor teacher.	3.3 Evaluate progress.	4.3 Hold hearing.
1.4 Evaluate progress.	2.4 Review and validate plan.		4.4 Action of board or hearing body.
	2.5 Initiate performance improvement plan.		4.5 Prepare for possible appeal.
	2.6 Monitor progress and evaluate for improvement.		

Adapted with permission from *ERS*, 1(2):18 (Summer 1983).

procedural and substantive due process requirements in dismissal cases see Frase and Downey (Forthcoming).

In summary, following due process is crucial to success and must be followed. Second, the process is much more likely to end in success when the administrator approaches the problem with the intent to assist the teacher until such time that it is clear that improvement is exceedingly unlikely and the only reasonable alternative is to recommend termination of employment.

1.2–The first question to answer after a performance problem has been detected is what does the deficiency stem from? Is the teacher's poor performance a managerial or organizational shortcoming? Are teaching supplies inadequate in quantity or quality? Are too many duties assigned?

The second question is whether or not the problem is a personal weakness of the teacher, and if so, is the deficiency due to lack of skill or effort? The former is a matter of training, the latter is a matter of attitude. These demand very different types of remediation. The following questions will help determine whether the problem is skill or effort deficiency.

- Could the teacher do what is expected if motivated to do so? (If life depended on it?)
- Has the teacher ever shown in the past that he or she is able to do what is expected?

If the answers to these questions are yes, the deficiency reflects a lack of motivation or effort. If the answers are no, the deficiency is likely due to a lack of skill.

Statements of deficiency, regardless of their nature, must be explicit and straightforward. Soft-soaping the problem will contribute to hindering the teacher's progress and will hurt the administrator's efforts in stages 2.0, 3.0, and 4.0.

Maintaining written records of all contacts with the teacher and all attempts to assist in improvement is crucial. It is easy to sluff off this chore. It takes time and it is a pain, but it is a key ingredient in the formula for success if the case proceeds to the hearing stage. Detailed, copious records are a must.

1.3–Efforts to correct deficiencies must be closely linked to the statements of deficiencies. Professional development at this time may consist of clinical supervision, collegial mentoring by a highly skilled teacher in the school, or observing and attending conferences with qualified mentors. The teacher in question should receive close attention during this step. This is not a witch hunt; instructional improvement is the goal. Keeping full records of these attempts on the administrator's part and anecdotal notes from MBWA activities is very important. Should the teacher not demonstrate sufficient improvement and the case goes to a hearing, the administrator *will* be called upon to show evidence of support given to the teacher.

1.4—This is a time for a close collegial relationship between the administrator, the teacher, and the mentor. It is important to remember that the teacher needs help and it is the administrator's job to give it. However, this spirit does not absolve the administrator of the responsibility to conduct a thorough and honest evaluation of the teacher's progress.

Deciding to drop the process or continue on to step 2.1 is sometimes difficult for an administrator to sort out. A few probing questions (see page 109) that deal with competence, management effort, and contamination of the system can help here.

The following questions are also helpful in making the go/no-go decision.

(1) Does the individual know he/she is marginal?

(2) How does the district justify keeping marginal employees?

(3) What is the *realistic* probability that the situation will improve?

If sufficient progress is demonstrated and if the answers to the above questions warrant it, the process stops here, if not, go on to 2.1.

2.0—This phase is more structured and formal than phase 1.0, and the requirements for keeping accurate records and maintaining a "helping" attitude are even more important.

2.1—Informing the assistant superintendent and legal counsel is advised at this time. Nothing rankles central office administrators more than being informed at the last minute that you want to present a dismissal decision to the board of education. Informing the supervisor from the beginning will prevent surprises and help insure cooperation. The same is true for legal counsel. Keep counsel informed and allow her to give advice on due process, documentation requirements, timelines, etc. Missing just one detail could cause the case to be thrown out sometime down the road. Technicalities are a nuisance but can make or break the case.

JOB PERFORMANCE EVALUATION

NAME OF EMPLOYEE:_____

CIRCLE THE APPROPRIATE RESPONSE:

	MARGINAL		COMPETENT		VERY COMPETENT

COMPETENCE

	MARGINAL		COMPETENT		VERY COMPETENT
1. HOW WELL DOES THE INDIVIDUAL *CURRENTLY* ACCOMPLISH THE RESPONSIBILITY OF TEACHING. (IS OR IS THIS PERSON NOT A COMPETENT TEACHER?)	1	2	3	4	5

MANAGEMENT EFFORT

	MORE THAN AVERAGE		AVERAGE		LESS THAN AVERAGE
1. HOW MUCH MANAGEMENT EFFORT DOES IT TAKE TO ENABLE THE INDIVIDUAL TO FUNCTION AT HIS/HER MOST EFFECTIVE LEVEL? (IS THIS PERSON A RESOURCE FOR THE SCHOOL OR A DRAIN OF OTHERS' ENERGIES AND OTHER RESOURCES?)	1	2	3	4	5

CONTAMINATION

	NEGATIVELY		MIXED BAG		POSITIVELY
1. IN WHAT WAY DOES THE INDIVIDUAL'S BEHAVIOR (VERBAL AND NON-VERBAL) IMPACT THE SYSTEM? (DOES THIS PERSON GIVE HEALTHY STIMULATION TO THE SCHOOL OR CAUSE TROUBLE?)	1	2	3	4	5

IF YOUR TOTAL RATING FOR THE INDIVIDUAL IS BELOW NINE POINTS YOU ARE DEALING WITH A *MARGINAL* EMPLOYEE.

Reprinted from Pfeiffer, W. and L. D. Goldstein, eds. *The 1984 Annual: Developing Human Resources.* San Diego, CA:University Associates, Inc. (1984). Used with permission.

2.2–The teacher must be informed of the responsibility to develop a performance improvement plan. The mentor (see 2.3) and administrator may help, but it must be clear that development of the plan is primarily the teacher's responsibility. The plan should include objectives which state what is to be accomplished, outcomes desired, and the method of measuring performance. The plan should also include the remediation activities, deadlines, and assistance needed.

2.3–A mentor or resource teacher should be selected at this time. The function of this person is to assist the teacher in improvement efforts. The mentor should be capable of modeling the teaching techniques designated as deficiencies in the performance improvement plan. The mentor must also agree to allow the teacher to observe his classes, observe the teacher's classes, and meet and confer with the teacher to discuss performance. The role of the mentor should be specified in the performance improvement plan. Care must be taken to avoid stating or implying that the mentor will serve to evaluate the teacher's performance. Teachers typically feel uncomfortable with this responsibility and should not be burdened with it. Teacher evaluation is the responsibility of the administration, either the principal or another administrator in the district. The mentor's role is to aid the teacher's improvement efforts.

2.4–Review and validation of the performance improvement plan are the administrator's responsibility. The following guidelines are helpful in accomplishing this task.

- Does the plan flow from the written deficiencies?
- Do the activities fit the performance problems the teacher is experiencing?
- Are the activities and evaluation methods in each objective consistent?
- Is the plan challenging, realistic, worthwhile, and achievable?
- Given the assumption that the teacher possesses the potential, are the activities likely to improve the teacher's performance?

A frequent fatal mistake made at this point is to accept the teacher's responsibility for improvement. Statements such as "we're going to work on this together" put the monkey on the administrator's back. The administrator's monkey (responsibility) is to provide services and assistance. It is the teacher's responsibility to improve. Statements such as this one generally are made when the administrator feels uncomfortable and wants to soften the impact on the teacher. *The situation is difficult for the teacher; this fact must be accepted.* Communication from the administrator must be straightforward and honest. Anything less will make further dealing in the process more difficult for the teacher and school district.

Finally, both the teacher and administrator should sign the performance improvement plan; each should get a copy. Copies should also be sent to file, the building administrator's supervisor, and legal counsel. The teacher may choose to give a copy to the mentor. The teacher is free to distribute this information, however, the administration should not do so without legal advice.

2.5 – Follow the plan, make changes only when the teacher agrees, and keep accurate and complete records. The school administrators should be in the classrooms on MBWA missions frequently, at least ten times a week for thirty-minute segments. Bringing in another evaluator is advised at this time. This could be another administrator at the school, but an administrator from another school or the district office is recommended to avoid a charge of collusion.

Following the completion of the performance improvement plan, the teacher should be given the opportunity to try out the skills in question with the mentor teacher before the administrator conducts another formal visit.

2.6 – During the monitoring and evaluating phase the administrator should assure the following:

- Supervision is ample in scope and amount. In other words, the administrator must practice frequent MBWA with this teacher. Close, helpful supervision is required.
- Valuative data and notes are complete, well-documented, and properly recorded.
- Assistance is provided per the performance improvement plan and properly documented.
- Teacher is treated fairly, equitably, and in a helpful professional manner.

Even though this stage of the process is designed to remedy the teacher's deficiencies, the administrator must anticipate the possibility that the teacher will not demonstrate adequate improvement and prepare accordingly. The preparation must include development of a *pattern* of inadequate performance. Single examples of ethical failure (molestation, physical abuse, etc.) are an exception, but a pattern of inadequate performance sustained over a period of time is necessary in preparation for a dismissal hearing on the basis of technical, bureaucratic, productive, or personal failure. The importance of a demonstrable history of inadequate practices is highlighted in the following statement by a judge in the Appellate Court of Illinois, Third District.

> Proof of momentary lapses in discipline or of a single day's lesson gone awry is not sufficient to show cause for dismissal of a tenured teacher. . . . Yet, where brief instances and isolated lapses occur repeatedly, there emerges a pattern of behavior which, if deficient, will support the dismissal of a tenured teacher. Where the school board fails . . . to show that the examples of conduct constitute a pattern of deficiency, then dismissal cannot be permitted. *Board of Education v. Ingels*, 394 N.E. 2d 69 (1979).

The most commonly used sources of valuative information are supervisors' evaluations based on classroom observations, anecdotal notes from MBWA, complaints from parents and students, and evaluations from students. Evaluations from students may be criterion-referenced instruments or norm-referenced instruments such as the Purdue Teacher Evaluation Scale. These scales should be administered by numerous teachers in the school to form a basis for local comparison. Local comparisons are needed for nationally normed instruments such as the Purdue. Parent and student evaluations must serve as supportive evidence, not as the major charge of incompetence. The strongest evidence of a teacher's incompetence is the supervisor's evaluation.

The golden rule in writing documentation is "always be factual." Documentation must be clear, direct, and relevant, and build a foundation of facts, not generalized conclusions (Rudd and Woodford, 1989).

The decision to stop the process or move on to phase 3.0 must be made on the basis of the *extent to which improvement in performance has been achieved and documented, not perceptions or the degree to which the teacher has "tried."* If sufficient improvement has not been made as stated in the performance plan, the decision to move to phase 3.0 must be made.

The decision should be discussed with the supervisor and reviewed by counsel before being given to the teacher.

3.0—By this time news of the teacher's performance and tenuous employment with the district is buzzing about the school and community. These are very trying times for the teacher, the administrator, and everyone else involved. The official notification given in this phase requires board action and is therefore public information in most states. This means exposure in the media. The authors have experienced this firsthand. In one instance, official notice of the board's charges against a teacher appeared in the local paper. Based on the calls received from the community, this was tantamount to heresy, let alone being highly insensitive and immoral. These complaints were made by a few parents who frequently complained about the teacher in question. No amount of explaining that "public" action was required by law would satisfy the parents. So it goes, sometimes criticism comes just as you are doing your utmost to ensure a quality education for students. The decision to recommend such action to the board wasn't made because the parents complained; it was made because the teacher's performance was well below standards. The action was in the best interests of the students.

It is reasonable to assume that the possibility of dismissal will hurt and anger a teacher. These emotions may be manifested in charges that the evaluations are invalid, in general irritability and in uncooperativeness. Resenting the teacher's anger complicates the situation and is ill-advised. Administrators must understand the origin of the stress, be compassionate, and remain firm in their decision to follow through with the process.

3.1—At this step, official notice of intent to recommend dismissal to the board of education if specific improvements are not made must be given to the teacher. The notice should be delivered by certified mail or by hand. If delivered by hand, a witness should be present to sign a document saying that the notice was received by the teacher, that the teacher refused to accept it, or whatever else may occur. This letter or official memorandum should be signed by the superintendent and approved by legal counsel to insure compliance with the law. The notice should state that a plan of corrective action (performance improvement plan) is being instituted because performance deficiencies have persisted through previous phases despite efforts by the administration to correct them. The following should be included in attachments to the notice.

(1) Statement of *specific* deficiencies

(2) Statement of *specific* corrections required

(3) Statement of *specific* criteria and instruments, if any, to be used in judging performance

(4) Statement of the improvement plan including activities for the teacher to engage in, important times and deadlines including the dates when the improvement plan will terminate and a final decision will be made, school or district assistance to be extended including names of persons to work with the teacher, number of professional leave days, and material resources

(5) Copy of appropriate statutes, past evaluations, pertinent district policies, and other information required by state law

3.2–Implement and conduct a plan. Carrying out the plan requires a good deal of time. Allowance for this demand must be planned and scheduled on the calendar in permanent ink. This is not something that can be stacked on top of everything else on the calendar; some other activities must be reassigned or postponed.

3.3–Stepping up the supervision schedule may be interpreted by the teacher as harassment. This is good reason for stating the supervision schedule very clearly in the notice. Teachers often claim harassment during hearings before the board or other hearing bodies. Monitoring should adhere to the schedule given in the notice and, again, detailed records should be kept of all activities related to the performance improvement plan.

Numerous evaluations should occur by more than one administrator *after* completion of the plan. Numerous visits per the MBWA plan should also take place while the plan is being carried out.

The final decision must be made on "performance" in relation to the deficiencies cited in the notice. This is another hard decision, but maintaining an awareness of the fact that the purpose of this exercise is *to ensure that only competent teachers are in contact with students* makes it rational, if not easier. It is the authors' experience and that of the nation's schools and businesses in general that the majority of these cases are referred on to the fourth phase for termination. This is not unexpected or unreasonable. We refer back to the 10 percent success rate for those who have initially been judged deficient in any career field. Not everyone employed by a school district as a teacher is destined to be a competent teacher. Teaching takes a special person with special skills. It is an insult to the profession to think that anyone can or should teach in the public schools.

Guidelines for conducting the termination phase are addressed in phase 4.0.

4.0—Administrators have two responsibilities in phase 4.0: (1) assisting in preparation for the hearing and (2) participating in the hearing.

4.1—The official notice of intent to terminate should be written by legal counsel. Statement of the intent, the charges, and the timeline will be included along with necessary documentation such as the evaluations, statutes, etc. Other requirements as stated in step 3.1 apply here also.

4.2—Preparing for the hearing involves development of the evaluation summary. The person assigned to this task varies from district to district. In large districts the director of personnel usually performs this function. In smaller districts the superintendent or assistant superintendent may draw the duty. Legal counsel will give direction for determining the contents and format of the summary and may also be called upon to write the summary. It is important to work closely with legal counsel in this effort to ensure the file is interpreted correctly. It is the authors' experience that lawyers, although most valuable during the process, are prone to overlooking key points regarding competence or pushing their legal interpretations to the point that the case is significantly weakened or misconstrued. Lawyers are paid to make interpretations; push them to justify their interpretations and do not give them carte blanche authority. Use them as advisers. The administration is responsible for the district and the outcome of the hearing. Authority must always accompany the person with the responsibility. The summative evaluation is a comprehensive and meticulous compilation of *all* valuative data in the teacher's file for the past three to five years and a description of the events occurring during the four-phase process.

The hearing will be a trying time for everyone involved. It will be necessary for the attorney to interview and coordinate with parents, teachers, administrators, and others who may become witnesses for the teacher. Purposes of the interview may be to help put them at ease, gain a more complete picture of the case, coordinate testimony, and anticipate questions from the teacher's attorney.

Deadlines for issuing notices vary from state to state, but the four-phase process in the case of a tenured teacher will take a full year. Meeting each deadline in the process is a must. Missing one can result in termination of the process and loss of the case. Timelines may be obtained from the state administrator's association, state school board association, district personnel office, or from legal counsel. Each administrator should keep a timeline in his office.

4.3 – A hearing officer (judge, board president, etc.) runs the hearing. The district's legal counsel runs the case for the district, and the school administrator supports legal counsel and offers advice when appropriate.

4.4 – The school administrator has no role at this step other than waiting and gearing up mentally for step 4.5.

4.5 – If the decision of the hearing office is in favor of the district, the teacher may have the right to an appeal, depending on state law. If appeal is a possibility, the school administrator, legal counsel, and personnel director or other central office administrator should begin preparing for an appeal. Transcripts of the hearing, testimony of witnesses, arguments posited by the defense, and the district's arguments must be reviewed and evaluated for strengths and weaknesses.

TENURE, DUE PROCESS, AND PROPERTY AND LIBERTY INTERESTS

Termination of teachers' contracts fall within two categories: dismissal and nonrenewal. Dismissal is the termination of employment during the term of a contract, nonrenewal is the act of not extending (renewing) a contract for the year following the current contract.

In the case of tenured teachers, termination of employment falls in the dismissal category in most states and requires due process. Due process is required because the tenured teacher has an expectancy of continued employment, not only through the remainder of the contract year, but also through the following years. This is considered a "property" or "liberty" interest and is the provision which separates tenure from nontenure. Contracts for tenured teachers cannot be "nonrenewed" due to these interests. "Cause" must be shown in cases involving termination of tenured teachers.

Termination of nontenured teachers can occur by dismissal or nonrenewal. Dismissal proceedings are generally pursued for bureaucratic, ethical, and, sometimes, personal failures which warrant immediate dismissal. In these cases the teacher represents an immediate danger to the students, other staff, or the school. Charges regarding technical, productive, or personal failure fall into the nonrenewal category. Nontenured teachers have a right to due process in the case of dismissal because they have expectations of employment through the length of the contract. They have no or significantly reduced rights to due process in the case of nonrenewal because they have no expectation to continued employment beyond the term of their current contract. Nontenured teachers have no property or liberty interests beyond the immediate contract. Therefore, the extensive four-phase process is not needed in the nonrenewal of a nontenured teacher's contract.

Most states grant tenure when the fourth full-time contract is signed. Some states such as California grant tenure with the third full-time contract. Regardless, nonrenewal of nontenured teachers is less rigorous than nonrenewal of tenured personnel in that demonstration of "cause" is either not required or is much less difficult. Following the timelines and due process procedures, however, is as important in nonrenewal of nontenured teachers as in cases involving tenured teachers. Arizona law is used as an example. Notice of intent not to renew a contract must be approved by the board of education and given to the teacher by January 15. This is called the ninety-day notice. The notice informs the teacher that he has ninety days to meet district performance standards. If the required improvement in performance is not observed by the end of the ninety-day period, the board acts to inform the teacher in writing that a contract will not be extended past the period designated in the current contract between the teacher and the district.

Property or liberty interests can be created by the board in its policies or by the state in statutes. Where these interests exist, the teacher has a right to due process, and the lengthy and expensive four-phase process is required. The implications of creating a policy which grants property or liberty interests are obvious and should be avoided since they restrict the administration's and board's authority to make decisions in the best interests of students.

KEY SUMMARY POINTS

(1) Keep in mind the administration's number one goal: putting only competent or better teachers in contact with students.

(2) When teacher deficiencies are detected, the first responsibility of the administration is to provide assistance to the teacher. Personal or ethical failures such as child abuse are exceptions to this rule. In these cases, the teacher must be at least temporarily barred from the classroom.

(3) Know the due process requirements, both procedural (e.g., rights to a hearing and notice) and substantive (fairness of the law).

(4) Due process provisions may be found in statutory laws and regulations, school board policies, state personnel commission policies, teachers' contract, and case law. Be familiar with these provisions.

(5) Know whether or not board policy grants "just cause" provisions to nontenure teachers. These provisions put the district in the position of being required to conduct lengthy and costly termination proceedings.

(6) Know the law and district policy.

(7) Tougher and more thorough evaluations and supervision are required as the four-phase process proceeds.

(8) Compile accurate and appropriate information only.

(9) Schedule adequate time for MBWA and other responsibilities related to the four-phase process.

(10) Keep comprehensive and accurate records of all activities and contacts regarding the process.

(11) Keep the central office administration and legal counsel well-informed.

(12) Allow the teacher reasonable time for improvement.

(13) Be consistent and fair in dealings with the teacher.

(14) Seek and scrutinize advice from legal counsel.

(15) Ensure that just cause or property and liberty interests are avoided in board policy.

Tackling a dismissal case is no small challenge and the rumors of tenure's sanctity have flourished and grown venerable over the years. Principals and supervisors sometimes think that their evaluations carry no weight. In situations where the evaluations are adequately documented, fair, based on classroom observations, and demonstrate a pattern of incompetency, this perception is groundless. Courts and hearing officers do give deference to supervisor's ratings and evaluations as reflected in the following opinion expressed by one judge:

> Teaching is an art as well as a profession and requires a large amount of preparation in order to qualify one in that profession. The ordinary layman is not well versed in that art, neither is he in a position to measure the qualifications required for the teacher of today. In our judgement this information can be imparted by one who is versed and alert in the profession and aware of the qualifications required. . . . We think the principal with the years of experience possessed by him can be classed properly as an expert in the teaching profession, and is in a similar position as a doctor in the medical profession. Fowler v. Young, et al., Board of Education, 65 N.W. 2d 399.

ALTERNATIVES TO THE DISMISSAL PROCESS

Alternatives to conducting the four-phase dismissal process are presented below, but none includes the option of leaving an incompetent teacher in the classroom. They all accomplish the required end of removing the incompetent teacher from contact with students.

1. Reassignment. Large districts may have positions for which the incompetent teacher is qualified and can perform adequately. In the past this alternative has suffered excessive use in the case of both incompetent teachers and administrators. If the teacher's skills and abilities match those required by the position, the reassignment is valid. If it is a way of avoiding biting the bullet, it is not valid. Reassigning incompetent teachers and administrators to new positions where their performance is also inadequate has given this alternative a black eye. Use only where appropriate.

2. Buy-Out. Terminating a tenure teacher or dismissing a temporary teacher costs money and taxes the energy of personnel. The buy-out plan can serve both the teacher and the district. The

teacher gains severance funds and avoids the embarrassment of going through the process. The buy-out can cost the district no more than the four-phase process and does not require the extensive efforts involved in the dismissal procedure. This option is particularly useful in cases where the district's argument is valid but for whatever reason may be in jeopardy at the hearing level or where the district would prefer to avoid the publicity generated by the process. In other cases, the third option is more viable.

3. Retirement. Teachers seldom want to choose to pursue the termination process, have their names in the paper, and the charges in their files. This is particularly true in the case of nonrenewal of nontenure teachers where there is little or no hope that they could win the case. In order to avoid the charges and to keep the files clean, resignation may be offered as a good alternative.

It is reasonable to expect that any administrator reading this chapter has just posited the weary queries: IS IT WORTH IT? DOES IT WORK? CAN WE REALLY DISMISS TENURED TEACHERS? Today, the answer is yes. Managing the marginal or incompetent teacher takes time, taxes emotions, induces psychological stress, and engenders feelings of self-doubt and guilt. It is no wonder that many principals have avoided confronting these teachers. But, yes, it can be done and it is worth it, for many good reasons. Weeding out the incompetents will have immediate impact on the quality of the school, such as improved test scores, and will result in greater respect from the public. The Catalina Foothills School District in Tucson, Arizona, and The Lake Washington School District in Kirkland, Washington, are perfect examples. The Catalina Foothills School District recently removed twenty-five incompetent teachers. The result was doubling or tripling of the percentage of students scoring in stanines 7–9. Community pride in the schools has grown immeasurably. The Lake Washington District removed eighty-nine incompetent teachers from 1979–1985. During this time, test scores increased from the 50 to 99th percentile. Parents are much happier with the schools.

The teacher is the most important factor in the educational process, and it is the administrator's responsibility to put the very best teachers available in contact with students. The difficulties appear imposing. They are not insurmountable. The replacement of truly incompetent teachers offers tremendous potential for greatly improving schools, student achievement, and public confidence.

Detecting incompetencies requires administrators to be out and about practicing the art of MBWA. Removing incompetents or watching and helping them become competent not only improves educational opportunities for students but makes MBWA more fun, pleasant, and rewarding because it is the right thing to do for students. After all, watching and helping a crackerjack teacher is a positive experience; watching an incompetent teacher isn't.

REFERENCES

ACHESON, K. A. and M. D. Gall. *Techniques in the Clinical Supervision of Teachers. Preservice and Inservice Applications*, 2nd ed. New York:Longman, Inc. (1987).

BOLAND, D. L. and S. L. Sims. "A Comprehensive Approach to Faculty Evaluation," *Jour. Nurs. Educ.*, 27:354–358 (October 1988).

BRACEY, G. W. "The Principal/Principle?" (Impact of Principals on Schools; Research by Perry Zirkel and Scott Greenwood). *Phi Delta Kappan*, 69:689 (May 1988).

BRACEY, G. W. "Teacher Efficacy and Student Outcomes," (Research by T. Guskey). *Phi Delta Kappan*, 69:526–527 (March 1988).

[a]BRIDGES, E. M. *The Incompetent Teacher*. Philadelphia:The Falmer Press (1985).

[b]BRIDGES, E. M. "Managing the Incompetent Teacher—What Can Principals Do?" *NASSP Bulletin*, pp. 58–59 (February 1986).

BRYANT, M. T. "Teacher Evaluation and Diminishment of Creativity," *Planning and Changing*, 19:36–40 (Spring 1988).

BUSER, R. L. and V. D. Pace. "Personnel Evaluation: Premises, Realities and Constraints," *NASSP Bull.*, 72:84–87 (December 1988).

CONLEY, D. R. "District Performance Standards: Missing Link for Effective Teacher Evaluation," *NASSP Bull.*, 72:78–83 (November 1988).

FRANKS, A. H. "Disclosure of Tenure Evaluation Materials," *Academe*, 74:36–37 (November/December 1988).

FRASE, L. E. and C. Downey. "Teacher Dismissal. Crucial Procedural Guidelines from Court Cases." Forthcoming in *National Forum of Applied Educational Research Journal*.

INMAN, L. and N. Tollefson. "Elementary Teachers' Attitudes Toward Preassessment Procedures," *Psychol. Sch.*, 25:331–337 (July 1988).

JOHNSON, S. *Teacher Unions in Schools*. Philadelphia:Temple University Press (1984).

KNOLL, M. *Supervision for Better Instruction: Practical Techniques for Improving Staff Performance*. Prentice-Hall (1987).

LANGLOIS, D. E. and M. R. Colarusso. "Improving Teacher Evaluation," *Educ. Digest*, 54:13–15 (November 1988) or *The Executive Educator*, pp. 32–33 (May 1988).

MURPHY, J. "Methodological, Measurement, and Conceptual Problems in the Study of Instructional Leadership," *Educ. Eval. Policy Anal.*, 10:17–39 (Summer 1988).

NEIL, S. B. and J. Custis. *Staff Dismissal: Problems & Solutions.* Arlington:American Association for School Administrators (1978).

NEWTON, E. H. and W. E. Braithwaite. "Teacher Perspectives on the Evaluation of Teachers," *Educ. Study*, 4(3):275–288 (1988).

ORDIORNE, G. Presentation at the Human Resource Development Conference, San Francisco, Sponsored by University Associates, Inc. San Diego, CA (March 1983).

PFEIFFER, W. Presentation at the Human Resource Development Conference, San Francisco, Sponsored by University Associates, Inc. San Diego, CA (March 1984).

PITKOFF, E. "RIF Without Wrath: The Personnel Function in Reductions in Force," *Am. Second. Educ.*, 17(2):15–19 (1988).

REDFERN, G. B. "Dismissing Unsatisfactory Teachers: A Four Phase Process," *ERS Spectrum*, 1(2):17–21 (1983).

REYNOLDS, B. J. and J. Martin-Reynolds. "Supervision Is the Key to Improving Instruction," *Am. Second. Educ.*, 1:2–5 (1988).

RUDD, R. C. and J. J. Woodford. *Supervisor's Guide to Documentation and File Building for Employee Discipline.* Crestline:Advisory Press (1989).

SCHACHTER, J. L. "Performance and Teacher Lay-Offs," *Int. Rev. Educ.*, 34(1):109–115 (1988).

SENDOR, B. "Know the Law Before You Fire or Frisk Someone," *AM Sch. Board Journal*, 175:8+ (January 1988).

SNYDER, W. R. and W. H. Drummond. "Florida Identifies Competencies for Principals, Urges Their Development," *NASSP Bull.*, 72:48–58 (December 1988).

STARRATT, R. J. "Administrative Leadership in Policy Review and Evaluation," *Educ. Eval. Policy Anal.*, 10:141–150 (Summer 1988).

SULLIVAN, R. L. and J. L. Wircenski. "Clinical Supervision: The Role of the Principal," *NASSP Bull.*, 72:34–36+ (October 1988).

TRACHTENBERG, S. J. "Teacher Competency: How Do We Assess It?" *Coll. Board Rev.*, 149:24–27 (Fall 1988).

WIDEEN, M. F. and I. Andrews, eds. *Staff Development for School Improvement: A Forum on the Teacher.* Falmer Press.

WILKS, B. and S. Sikes. "Guidelines to Practical Impact Evaluation," *Innov. Higher Educ.*, 13:54–65 (Fall/Winter 1988).

ZIMMERMAN, L. and J. Westfall. "The Development and Validation of a Scale Measuring Effective Clinical Teaching Behaviors," *Jour. Burs. Educ.*, 27:274–277 (June 1988).

CHAPTER VII

MBWA Essential Skills

HOW THE "GOOD" AND THE "NOT SO GOOD" PRINCIPALS USE THEIR TIME

MBWA takes time! The author knows of no administrator who claims to have time to spare. Furthermore, this person would not admit it if it were true. All administrators seem to have very busy schedules, but some administrators are already out on campus, in classrooms, on playgrounds, and in the hallways practicing MBWA. Research on effective schools has clearly and convincingly concluded that strong leadership is a key characteristic of effective schools. Leaders in effective schools are highly visible through frequent classroom visits, touring the campus, and asserting themselves in the instructional program. These leaders are out and about the school and classrooms keeping the school on target and helping in all phases of the program. The question is, if these administrators are spending two to four hours a day doing MBWA, what are the other administrators doing with their same two to four hours? Let's take a look.

The Association for Supervision and Curriculum Development (1987) offers comparisons and recommendations on how principals should spend their time (see page 124).

The *AVERAGE* principal spends 27 percent of his time on program improvement in comparison to the 41 percent spent by the *STRONG* principal. This discrepancy is reflected in the amount of time spent on managing buildings and student-related services. The average principal spends 67 percent of his time on these activities, while the strong leader devotes only 52 percent

JOB DIMENSIONS OF THE SCHOOL PRINCIPAL	AVERAGE (HOW THE AVE. PRINCIPAL SPENDS TIME)	STRONG LEADER (HOW STRONG LEADER SPENDS TIME)
A. Educational Programmatic Improvement	27%	41%
B. Community Relations	7%	7%
C. Student-Related Services and Activities	28%	18%
D. Building Mgmt. Operations and District Relations	39%	34%

of his time. Job dimensions A, B, and C, in particular, call for principals to be out of the office and with people, in other words, close to the classroom.

Separate studies by Howell (1981), Peterson (1977–78), Morris (1981), Martin and Willower (1981), Kmetz and Willower (1982) and Stronge (1988) reveal large variations in time allocated by principals.

WHERE	PERCENTAGE OF TIME
In the office area	40–80%
In hallways and on the grounds	10–23%
Off campus	11%
In classrooms	2.5–10%

A brief review quickly reveals a number of very important problems:

(1) Principals are spending up to 80 percent of their time in the office area. This leaves very little time for MBWA.

(2) More time is spent off campus than in classrooms. The studies by Martin and Willower (1981) and Kmetz and Willower (1982) found that principals spent only 2.5 percent of their time in classrooms and Stronge (1988) found that principals

spend only 6.2% of their time on instructional leadership. The 23 percent spent in hallways and on the grounds and 11 percent off campus is reasonable, but the 80 percent in the office area must be reduced to allow time for MBWA in general, specifically in classrooms. Principals are typically not pleased with the fact that so much time is spent in the office and recognize that it must be reduced (Valentine, Clark, Nickerson, and Keefe, 1981).

The significance of these problems is further magnified by the fact that the principal's accessibility, being out and about on campus and not locked up in an office, is not only highly correlated with leader effectiveness, but also serves to increase teachers' feelings of confidence, patience, and control. In addition, accessibility further enhances teacher–student relationships by increasing students' acceptance of advice and criticism, increasing students' involvement, and decreasing student discipline problems (Blaze, 1987). Further, as Andrews, Soder and Jacoby (1986) found, MBWA is also directly related to student achievement, particularly minority and low socio-economic students.

Later in this chapter, the "Office Time Wasters" will be identified and a plan will be provided for analyzing how you spend your time and how to free up your time for MBWA.

Some administrators plan their day to include MBWA activities such as classroom observation, teacher supervision, and even teaching, while others continue to spend the majority of the day checking out what is going on, serving as the school spokesperson, disseminating information to staff members, and handling disturbances (Morris et al., 1984). Research tells us that principals fail to spend more time in the classroom and less time in the office, even though they say they desire to do so and are given discretion to do so (see Hager and Scarr, 1983). Mere dissatisfaction with the status quo is unlikely to lead to change. Change requires an understanding—a vision of a well-run school, a desire to change, and plan for doing it. The ingredients for creating a plan are addressed in the following pages.

If the "vision" is formulated and backed by commitment, a very reasonable question is: "If my day is already filled, where am I going to find four hours for MBWA?" The answer is difficult, but not impossible or unreasonable. The first hurdle is withdrawal from the "quick fix" search. Like "get rich quick" schemes, quick fixes aren't worth a nickel. The world may treat us differently when it comes to heredity and inheritance, but time is distributed equitably, without financial cost and without bias. Each of us gets twenty-four hours per day. Yet some people accomplish a great deal *and* practice MBWA while others have excuses why they cannot get out of the office and are continually searching for *more* time–the quick fix. If a prophet extols the virtue of the "time making" machine to you and blames others for your lack of time, tell him to pedal his phoney nostrums elsewhere and implore him to face up to the fact that we all have the same amount, twenty-four hours a day and 365 days per year, and more cannot be manufactured. But days can be rearranged and organized to fit your demands.

TIME IN YOUR LIFE

The following pages offer a few simple techniques for making better use of time and managing it as a precious resource to allow you to practice MBWA and get the "other stuff" done also. Finding time for MBWA is a matter of values and attitudes and is not dependent on intellect. Buy into the idea that you can control your day and demands on your time and you're half there. The other half is found on the following pages. The ideas which follow do not comprise a magic elixir. They require effort, but they are not all that hard. Follow them and you'll have the time to be out on campus and in the classrooms.

A number of forms and checklists are provided throughout this chapter. We hope you will use the forms like a workbook. If you prefer not to write in the book, copy the forms and store them in a notebook for future reference. When you finish the chapter, you will have your own plan for finding time to MBWA. Let's get started.

The first step is to take a look at the big picture, all your time, not just the work day. It's commonly thought that there are eight life roles: personal, professional, family, community, social, cultural, recreational, and spouse. Each deserves attention and time. The exact amount of time is up to you, but the general view is that a well-rounded person participates in all eight areas. What is the relative value of each to you? The eight life roles are presented in Column 1 in Table 7.1. Rate the importance of each

TABLE 7.1 **Life role analysis.**

ROLES	PRIORITY RATING (1–5 HIGH)	TIME DEVOTED (HOURS)	DISCREPANCY (HOURS)
1. Personal			
2. Family			
3. Social			
4. Community			
5. Professional			
6. Cultural			
7. Recreational			
8. Spouse			

of these eight on a 1 (low) to 5 (high) scale, and write your ratings in the "Priority Rating" column. Take a few minutes with this and avoid assigning a "5" ranking to each. In the next column, "Time Devoted," write the number of hours you spend each week in each role. Now, examine your priorities and time spent on each. Do your time allocations match your priorities? If you rated Family as number one priority, did you also give it a large amount of time? If physical exercise is important to you, are you devoting time to it?

If you find discrepancies, and most of us do, write some goals and short-term activities (one-month time range) on a card (see Table 7.2) to reduce each discrepancy and use one card per discrepancy.

Next, pick one or two goals/discrepancies to work on first. Mark your activities on your calendar and do them. Don't feel guilty if your activities call for more time for something other than work. Work is not all of our lives and our lives should not be all work! Take time for the other roles. Take time to smell the roses! Effective leaders take time to reflect and relax; they work hard *and* play hard.

PLANS FOR REDUCING DISCREPANCIES

Now for freeing up time at work. Managing and controlling your time will help you do this. A good way to start is by clarify-

TABLE 7.2 Plans for reducing discrepancies.

LIFE ROLE:	Family
DISCREPANCY:	I value my family very highly and I spend only 3 hours per week with them.
GOAL 1.0:	Spend 4 hours more per week with immediate family.
ACTIVITIES:	1.1 Take kids to movie this Friday.
	1.2 Visit my folks on Wednesday evening.
	1.3 Eat with my kids and wife on Thursday night instead of staying at the office.
LIFE ROLE:	Personal
DISCREPANCY:	I engage in no aerobic exercise and should engage in 3 hours per week.
GOAL 2.0:	Spend 3 hours per week working out at the club.
ACTIVITIES:	2.1 Call for appointment with club trainer for Saturday morning.
	2.2 Set up 3-hour per week workout schedule and put on my calendar.

ing what time management isn't. A discussion of six common management myths follows.

TIME MANAGEMENT MYTHS

MYTH 1

The more time I spend at work, the more I will get done; more is better. Eventually, mental fatigue will occur or you get just plain tired. When either occurs, productivity goes down and your time is essentially wasted. A task that ordinarily takes fifteen minutes takes forty-five, and the quality is poor. Frequently you must revise and correct it the next day. This is neither efficient nor effective. In fact, it's inefficient and ineffective and a perfect scenario of diminishing returns.

> POINT—THE RELATIONSHIP BETWEEN TIME AND PRODUCTIVITY IS CURVI-LINEAR—INITIALLY, AS TIME GOES UP, PRODUCTIVITY GOES UP, BUT AFTER A POINT, PRODUCTIVITY GOES DOWN AS TIME GOES UP! DON'T PERSEVERATE AT A TASK!

MYTH 2

I operate with the open door policy. It's smart to greet everyone who comes into the office. Being open and visible is good policy and crucial to good PR. Aristotle's Golden Mean applies here— *EVERYTHING IN MODERATION*. Seeing, greeting and chatting with everyone that comes through the office doors isn't moderation. People like seeing the administration head, but if they see you on every occasion, they may start to wonder if you do anything other than operate the "glad hand."

POINT—TAKE TIME TO GREET PEOPLE BUT TAKE TIME FOR OTHER DUTIES TOO. START BY ORGANIZING YOUR TIME AND PLAN TO CLOSE THE DOOR FOR SPECIFIC PERIODS TO GET YOUR PAPERWORK DONE, MAKE CALLS, AND MAKE PLANS FOR MBWA.

MYTH 3

The principal's job is very important; I had better do it all myself. Nonsense, the top executives of America's top corporations don't do it all. The best leaders hire capable people and delegate tasks to them. More than delegating tasks, they also delegate responsibility and autonomy to get the job done. Teachers who are ready for the challenge can benefit from job enrichment. New responsibility and autonomy will give them new life and enthusiasm for their job. Blaze (1987) reported that delegation of authority was not only associated with effective performance but also resulted in increasing teachers' self-esteem and sense of professionalism, morale, and efficiency. Credentialed and certified people (administrators, in other words) are not the only capable people. Chances are that a number of very capable parents and teachers would respond most favorably to the opportunity to "head up" many of the functions that go on in our schools. Assess their ability, plan with them, and give them the reins.

POINT—YOU'RE RESPONSIBLE FOR THE ORGANIZATION, BUT YOU CAN'T DO IT ALL, SO DON'T TRY—DELEGATE.

MYTH 4

I just don't have the time for it with all the expectations placed on me. Who's in control? Who is running the ship? All those others placing demands on you? The personality variable known as locus of control offers insight here. At one end of the locus of control continuum is the internal person and at the other is the external person. The internal believes that he or she can control fate while the external believes that his or her life is controlled by external factors such as fates, spirits, powers, and significant others. Those who believe that they have impact on their destiny (internals) are more likely to act that way. They are more likely to stop smoking, start exercising, and wear their seat belts. Externals, on the other hand, do not engage in these measures. If I get lung cancer, if I'm thrown against the dash of the car in a fender bender, or if I get flabby and my heart is overtaxed, that's just the way it is. Well, the fact is that you can be in control and you *should* be in control. Let people know you can't do everything and that they may have to do something if they want it done; that includes your boss. Learn to say no.

POINT—YOU'RE RESPONSIBLE FOR YOUR ORGANIZATION, TAKE CONTROL AND RUN IT; START WITH YOUR TIME.

MYTH 5

I must read my mail—all of it. If 60 percent of your mail never reached you, you would be no worse off and would never miss it. Like the mail we receive at home, much of the mail to administrators is sales literature. Leave it alone or deep six it. If you needed it, you would already have known it. Reading the stuff just creates "wants." After developing a want you may buy it. A want created by a sales brochure is often destined to occupy space on the shelf, never to be used. Time spent reviewing the literature, placing the order, and leafing through it after it arrives costs the organization $50.00 or more in personnel time and costs you from twenty minutes to an hour of your precious time. More about handling mail later.

POINT—DON'T LET THE MAIL CONTROL YOU—CONTROL IT!

MYTH 6

Some problems will just go away if I pay no attention to them. Besides, I really don't have time now to deal with it. There are two points here. The first is a matter of semantics. Sometimes we perceive things as problems when they really aren't. These will go away and we shouldn't devote time to them. But if a problem exists, acting like an ostrich won't help. Problems must be dealt with, otherwise they fester and spread throughout the organization. If you thought the problem would take too much time when it first presented itself, it will take four times that much time later.

POINT—THE OSTRICH'S PROBLEMS DON'T GO AWAY WHEN HE STICKS HIS HEAD IN THE SAND AND NEITHER WILL YOURS. SPEND ONE HALF HOUR NOW AND SAVE FOUR HOURS DOWN THE ROAD!

IDENTIFYING TIME WASTERS

Those are some of the myths. Now get started on your plan for more effective use of time so that you can accommodate MBWA. Everyone has the same amount of time each day, twenty-four hours, and each of us wastes some of our allotment. Some of us waste more than others. Time wasters have been studied for many years, and some very useful lists have been developed. After studying corporate presidents, vice presidents and board presidents, Powers (1965) identified the ten worst time wasters:

(1) Telephones
(2) Mail
(3) Meetings
(4) Public relations
(5) Paperwork
(6) Commuting
(7) Business lunches
(8) Civic duties
(9) Incompetents
(10) Family demands

Mackenzie (1972), in an international study of managers, identified fifteen leading time wasters:

(1) Telephone interruptions
(2) Drop-in visitors
(3) Meetings—scheduled as well as unscheduled
(4) Crisis situations for which planning ahead was not possible
(5) Lack of objectives, priorities, or deadlines
(6) Cluttered desks and personal disorganization

(7) Involvement in routine and detail that should be delegated

(8) Attempting too much at one time and underestimating the time it takes to do it

(9) Failure to set up clear lines of responsibility and authority

(10) Inadequate, inaccurate, or delayed information from others

(11) Indecision and procrastination

(12) Lack of clear communication and instruction

(13) Inability to say no

(14) Lack of standards and progress reports—accountability

(15) Fatigue

Time wasters are essentially of two types: internal and external. Drop-in visitors, telephone calls, meetings called by others, addressing the needs of others are examples of external time wasters. Internal time wasters come from us, the person in charge, and frequently appear in the form of procrastination, handling the same paper four times instead of once, not planning the day or week, not saying "no" when you really should, trying to do everything yourself, and not discriminating between tasks in terms of importance and value. Here is where Parato's dreaded 80/20 law bites us again: 20 percent of our decisions account for 80 percent of the results. The key is to focus on those 20 percent that yield big results. When we devote 80 percent of our time to time wasters we are not being productive, and we are not accomplishing the "big" results. If we do not focus on them, they just won't get done or at least not to the level required and desired.

PLANNING FOR MORE EFFECTIVE USE OF TIME

Time wasters are the enemy and must be eliminated, or at least significantly reduced. Before we can declare war on them we must know what and who "them" is. Table 7.3 is designed to do just that. Make a copy of it and get started. Common administrative activities are listed on the horizontal axis in columns A–P. Write in your unique activities in lines Q–W. You will be using this list to analyze your day and identify your time wasters, so add your typical daily, weekly, and monthly activities to the list so that it "fits you."

The vertical column is divided into fifteen-minute time periods. Fifteen-minute segments may seem excessively small, but Sproul's (1976) study of managers revealed that the average length of an activity was only nine minutes, and Morris et al. (1984) found that face to face contacts range from five minutes and twenty seconds to two minutes and thirty seconds per contact. The frequency of contacts is further exacerbated by interruptions, which occur at a rate of 1.7 per task (Kmetz and Willower, 1982). If anything, fifteen minutes is too *infrequent*. Should you find that the fifteen-minute segments do not work for you, record your data more frequently. Every fifteen minutes, check the appropriate column to indicate the activity(s) for that period. An "I" (for internal) or "E" (for external) should be placed in Column X to record whether the activity was initiated by you or someone else: "I" for self-initiated and "E" for other-initiated. Next, place a "P" (for planned) or "U" (for unplanned) in Column Y for each activity. Last, rate each activity in terms of its importance and write the rating in Column Z. Use a five-point scale with five being highly important and one being unimportant. Keep the log for two consecutive days. Record the totals for each column at the bottom.

I know, this analysis takes time but you will get right into it, and it won't seem like an inconvenience. Consider it an investment! For instance, Blaze (1987) found that teachers in schools where principals managed their time effectively experienced decreases in feelings of frustration, increases in productive faculty meeting interactions, and both students and teachers experienced decreases in time wasted. Time-management will pay big dividends. It takes time to save time, and the initial investment will pay benefits well into the future.

Now that you have recorded your week's activities and have the totals, analyze the data. Start with the following questions.

What percentage of my activities were planned? The acceptable range is 60–80 percent. If your percentage is not between 60 percent and 80 percent go to the next question—How important do you perceive the unplanned activities to be? Which activities account for most of your unplanned activity? Circle these in red and record them in Column A of Table 7.4, if the relative importance rating is less than 4. These activities are likely to be telephone calls, meetings, and drop-in visits. A little later we will make plans for cutting back on these.

TABLE 7.3 Principal activity record: or what I did today!

ACTIVITY:	A	B	C	D	E	F	G	H	I	J	K	L	M	N	O	P	Q	R	S	T	U	V	W	X	Y	Z
	Telephone	Mail	Meetings—Parents	Meetings—District Office	Meetings—School Staff	Reports	Lunch	Civic Duty	Drop-in Visitor	Discipline—Student	Classroom Observation	Directing Office Staff	Curriculum/Instruction	Planning the Day/Week	Dealing with Emergency	Resting								I or E	P or U	1 to 5
7:15																										
7:30																										
7:45																										
8:00																										
8:15																										
8:30																										
8:45																										
9:00																										
9:15																										
9:30																										
9:45																										
10:00																										
10:15																										
10:30																										
10:45																										
11:00																										
11:15																										
11:30																										
11:45																										
12:00																										
12:15																										
12:30																										

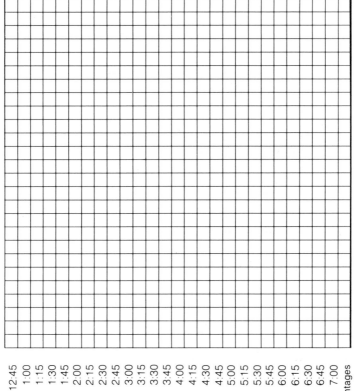

12:45
1:00
1:15
1:30
1:45
2:00
2:15
2:30
2:45
3:00
3:15
3:30
3:45
4:00
4:15
4:30
4:45
5:00
5:15
5:30
5:45
6:00
6:15
6:30
6:45
7:00

Totals and Percentages

TABLE 7.4 **Activity analysis or: separating the wheat from the chaff.**

	"A" UNIMPORTANT UNPLANNED ACTIVITIES	"B" UNIMPORTANT NOT INITIATED BY ME
1.		
2.		
3.		
4.		
5.		
6.		
7.		
8.		
9.		
10.		
11.		
12.		
13.		
14.		
15.		
16.		
17.		
18.		
19.		
20.		

Next question—What percentage of your activities was initiated by someone other than you? The ideal is 20 percent for someone else and 80 percent for you. Note which activities are being initiated by someone else and circle them. Are more than 20 percent of your activities being initiated by someone or something else? If so, go to the next question—How important do you perceive them to be? Record those unplanned activities with an importance rating of less than 4 in Column B of Table 7.4. The biggest invaders are likely to be uninvited telephone calls, drop-in visits, and paperwork from the state or district office.

Do some unplanned activities with importance ratings of less than 4 appear in both columns? Your answer is likely to be yes! There they are, the triple threat team, unplanned by you, uninitiated by you, and unimportant to you, taking your time. Go ahead, be outraged! They have taken your time from MBWA or reading that book you've been hoping to get to. Remember, the eight life roles discussed a few pages ago? You may have just found the time for balancing them out and creating a more healthy lifestyle and practicing MBWA.

TIME-MANAGEMENT STRATEGIES

Here are some time-management strategies for reducing or even eliminating the big four triple threat time wasters: TELEPHONES, DROP-IN VISITORS, MAIL, AND MEETINGS. Read the following strategies for dealing with the big four.

TOO MUCH TIME ON THE TELEPHONE

There are two possible problems here: too many phone calls and too much time per call. Who initiated the calls? If they are being initiated by someone other than you, structure the time you will devote to returning calls; maybe a half hour before lunch and a half hour in the afternoon. Before lunch is a good time because people tend to be brief when lunch is waiting. This will give you time to engage in "outside the office" activities like MBWA and evaluating staff.

True emergency calls are another story—take them. Also, remember that definitions of emergency differ for parents, principals, board members, and superintendents. Train your secretary to discriminate and give only the emergencies to you. The cardinal rule is to return all calls. Set aside time each day for this. The parents will love it when you return the call later in the afternoon and will consider you a very considerate person for taking the time to do so. Also, their problem may have shrunk just a little bit and be easier to resolve.

Make a list of calls that you must make and prioritize them. Start with the most important and use a timer. Set the timer at three minutes to keep you on schedule. When time is up say, "Joan, I have a bunch of calls to return so I better move on." Being put on hold is a time waster, so don't let it happen. If for some reason you feel it is necessary, have work organized on your desk so that you can be productive while waiting. A conference phone works wonders here; it frees your hands to do other things. Chit-chatting on the phone is also a big time waster. Be mindful of this; stick to the point. Be sure to set your timer. If the person you are talking with seems intent on rambling, use one of the following to bring the conversation to an end:

- "My appointment is waiting, Paul. I really must go."
- "Let's plan to get together regarding this idea, but I must go now."
- "John, it's been great talking with you but I must hang up so I can prepare for the superintendent's meeting."
- "My next appointment is waiting. I must go."

Sometimes you can treat the problem preventatively. When a call is initiated with a gabber, start off with "I have two minutes unscheduled and then I must run." If this doesn't work, your secretary can help here. Have her primed to interrupt when the conversation hits the two-minute mark.

TOO MANY DROP-IN VISITORS

Fact 1

Schools and school districts are service agencies and must serve the people of the community and affiliated organizations.

Fact 2

You do not always have to serve at the drop of a hat and at others' convenience. Here are some ideas for controlling (reducing) the number of drop-in visitors.

(1) Position the secretary's desk so that she can screen visitors, answer questions that do not require your attention, route visitors to other qualified officials, take messages, or schedule appointments for you. Before implementing this strategy, be certain that the secretary understands the role and has the required skills. If you believe training is needed, check with

your central office staff development department, state administrators association, or local community college for training programs. These strategies can backfire, so be sure the secretary possesses all the skills needed to do the job. She is the first line of PR and can make you look like a hero or an insensitive dolt.

(2) Position your desk so that it is not visible from the outer office. Eye contact will invite passersby into your office. If they do not see you, they will be much less likely to drop in, unless they are particularly aggressive. That's where your secretary earns her money.

(3) Your office should promote comfortable and efficient meetings with your visitors without being too comfortable. Chairs should be straight, a bit hard, and definitely not plush. This will help keep the visitation to a reasonable length. Sometimes it is difficult for visitors to end the conversation. You can terminate the conversation with "closers" like "My next appointment is in two minutes and it's been great talking with you," or, "I'm sorry I don't have more time, but I hope to see you again." Movement toward the door will help deliver the message. Chairs are for planned guests. Unless you feel it very important, drop-in visitors should not be offered a chair. Remain standing. If you sit down, they will too. Give them two minutes, walk them to the door, thank them, and say goodby.

A large percentage of drop-in visitors are salespeople, and they are aggressive. Unless highly trained, the receptionist or secretary will succumb, pity them, bring them in to see you. This visit takes a half hour at least and up to an hour or more. The unknowing receptionist will say, "But he was very nice and seemed to have a great spelling series, so I thought you would want to see him." Wrong! You didn't and you don't want to see him. Not now, not ever, never! Unless you call him. Help your secretary or receptionist understand that you are not being unkind, you are simply doing your job. Share with her the fact that the Educational Sales Representatives' Association of Maryland, the District of Columbia, and Delaware listed 156 representatives in their 1979–80 directory (Shipman, 1983, p. 88) and that by now there's likely to be another 100+ out there looking for ways to occupy principals' time. A half hour drop-in visit from only 50 percent of them will take 65+ hours. You can't and shouldn't afford that much time. Tell your receptionist that you are not available on a drop-in basis. The author does not see salespeople at all unless we ask them in. If you need something, you'll know it; then call a salesman. Remember, few principals have been fired because salespeople think they are unkind, and few are ever promoted because they score in the 9th stanine on the salespersons' "how I feel about the principal" inventory.

Stay in control; time is a finite resource, so don't give five minutes away any faster than you would one hundred dollar bills.

Some bosses have ways of dropping in. They feel comfortable dropping into your office, dropping in through the phone, and dropping you into their meetings. They tend to have lots of ideas, and all of them take your time. We most assuredly advocate developing good rapport with your boss, but is he taking too much of your time with activities that significantly distract from your ability to keep your school at the level the district expects? If so, you have a problem and the monkey is on your back. Honesty is the best policy, and it is up to you to initiate the conversation. Here are the steps for you to follow in helping your boss get a grip on the effects of his demands so that you can do your job.

(1) List the unplanned jobs he gave to you this past week.

(2) Estimate the amount of time you devoted to these demands.

(3) List the tasks you were prepared to do this week.

(4) List those tasks from list 1 and 3 that you did not get done or did not get done to the same level of excellence you and the district expect.

(5) Put yourself in the boss's shoes. Are the demands really excessive? Can you juggle things to make it all happen?

(6) If you conclude that the demands are truly excessive and spending time on them will hurt the school, schedule a meeting with the boss. Highlight those tasks you planned to do but were displaced by his "unplanned" interruptions. Share with him the problem you are having.

(7) Share items 1–4 with him. Ask him/her if these reflect his expectations. Add others if appropriate.

(8) Get agreement on his/her expectations and the reality of the problem.

(9) Thank him and be sure to keep him/her updated on your activities.

This process takes a lot of tact. You will never be totally comfortable with the prospect of presenting such information to the boss—so don't expect it. If you do not know the boss well, it may be wise to confer with a trusted colleague about the problem and the meeting. Don't wait, do it!

THE MAIL TRAP

As we stated in Myth 5, if you never saw 60 percent of your mail, you would not have missed anything you couldn't live without. In-baskets, out-baskets, and other paraphernalia such as file folders can be helpful, but not necessarily for everyone. Simply putting a tray or two on your desk is not going to reduce your time spent on mail. Some people use them well: the trays serve as organizers for incoming and outgoing mail and those items that you want to let sit for a few days to prove their worth. The trays should be convenient to you and your secretary. The bottom tray is for incoming mail. Have the secretary deliver it to you in three groups: junk mail, correspondence, and immediate action. It will take you less than a minute to assess the value of the junk mail and funnel it to the round file. Ask the secretary to draft a nice "take me off your mailing list" form letter and send it to those who send you junk mail. Don't worry about missing something. When was the last time you were introduced to a great idea via the brochures and catalogues that constitute junk mail? The response is likely to be *NEVER*. Kmetz and Willower (1982) found that the second most frequent originator of principals' correspondence was vendors. Depend on others and a few tried and true publications to give you the hot ideas.

You should act on your correspondence immediately; otherwise, it simply builds. If the letter requires a response, dictate it then and there or belly up to your trusty word processor and pound out your response. If you need information before you can respond, attach a note and give it to the secretary. She may even be able to prepare the response. If someone else can act on the item, send it to them and note the action required. Spend fifteen minutes a day for three or four days training your secretary in the fine art of handling mail. Your secretary is a valuable asset and frequently can act as an administrative assistant. Let her use and expand her talents to save you time.

If you are in a quandary as to whether you should respond, ask yourself what will happen if you do not. Put it in a hold tray or ask someone else to give it back to you in one week. Most of these items will be forgotten. Learn to throw them away. Don't clutter your files with this stuff. If you find yourself ordering file cabinets each year, you are saving too much. There are no rewards for the principal, assistant superintendent, or superintendent "who has the highest volume of paper" in files. Make it one of your objectives; cut way back on the paper load.

Dictaphones can save the time traditionally spent waiting for the secretary to gather her note pad and pencil and get into your office; plus, you can talk faster than you can write. Mackenzie (1972) tells us that we generally write 20–30 words per minute while we can speak 150 words per minute. This can save time *and* it can waste time because we tend to become verbose when we talk into a machine. Transcribing tapes is a time waster for secretaries and you are responsible for saving their time too. Take a minute to organize your thoughts before you start talking and stick to the point. Using the word processor can save time over the dictaphone if you know how to type. It's been our experience that 70 percent of the memos dictated must be revised. That costs you and your secretary a lot of time. Seeing your work on a screen, knowing that if you make a mistake it can be easily corrected, and being able to move your sentences and rearrange your thoughts in a moment helps reduce the "revision" percentage to 10 percent. This is a time saver and tends to produce a higher quality communique.

The hand-held, microcassettes are very handy, help keep your thoughts organized, and serve as a failsafe memory. Use the recorder in your car or in the "field" for recording those notes and great ideas you can't afford to forget. When your secretary transcribes them, put them on your list of things to do or take whatever action is necessary. Sometimes you will just throw them away; they weren't so great as you thought.

MEETINGS: WASTING TIME VERSUS MAKING PROGRESS

Meetings take time. Doyle (1985, p. 4) estimates that managers sit through more than 9,000 hours of meetings in a lifetime; that's more than a full year. As your success goes up so does your time spent in meetings. Middle managers, such as principals, spend 35 percent of their time in meetings. Superintendents spend 50 percent+ in meetings. That means a very significant part, 35–50 percent, of your organizational life will be spent in meetings. With that kind of time commitment for higher paid personnel, Doyle (1985, p. 4) extrapolates that as much as 15 percent of the organization's budget may be spent on meetings.

When we hear of another meeting, we groan! When teachers hear of another meeting, they groan. So why are we having all these meetings? Can we and the organization do without them? The answer is "yes," sometimes. Schools are people organizations and people must meet in groups in order to accomplish some tasks. Without meetings some groups would wither and die. Some meetings are considered so important that legislators require them, e.g., school boards, boards of directors, boards of supervisors, and many others. Meetings are the most efficient and effective way to communicate information and solve problems. Organizational problems sometimes need group participation or input before an effective solution can be developed. Participation of the group equals involvement, involvement leads to ownership, ownership leads to cooperation, and cooperation leads to successful problem resolution.

The key is to have meetings when they are needed and not to have them when they are not needed. A few questions will help you weed out those not needed meetings. Meetings should not be held when:

(1) A memo or telephone call would accomplish the mission as effectively.

(2) Adequate preparation has not taken place.

(3) The subject is confidential and should not be shared with all members of a group.

(4) The subject simply does not warrant the time of those required to attend.

(5) It is a hot topic and people need time to simmer and calm down before they can work together in a collegial manner.

(6) It is simply routine.

Rule one is the most frequently broken. If the task is to "disseminate" information about schedules and routines, a memo will work just as well and will save the teachers and you time. I think we have all been in this type of meeting and just as we resented it, so do the teachers. They have better things to do with their time. If you are a superintendent, consider those monthly or weekly meetings you call. Unless you provide great entertainment and food, your principals would probably prefer spending their time at their schools taking care of business. These meetings may be the external force which wastes a good bit of their time. Principals, middle managers, and coordinators, if you have such a meeting on your calendar (team meetings, coordinator meetings, superintendent meetings) take action by not going. Be sure to cover bases. If the meeting is optional, call and ask forgiveness but do not attend. Do not misunderstand, we are not recommending insubordination; if it is required, go! If the meetings are required and they keep you from accomplishing important tasks, you may have to talk to your boss as discussed on page 140.

PLANNING FOR EFFECTIVE AND EFFICIENT MEETINGS

There are three basic types of meetings and each has a different purpose.

Information Oriented Meetings

These meetings are for sharing information. Examples are the final briefing before a big event at the school or a progress report or a new policy that is likely to elicit questions. If it is not likely to elicit questions, send it to the members in the school mail. If necessary, go over a few of the highlights at the next "necessary" meeting.

Action Oriented Meetings

When there is a need to discuss a problem, clear the air, or build esprit de corps, then a well-planned meeting is a must. Decision making is another very legitimate reason for having a meeting. In these meetings all participants share responsibility for:

- bringing and defining the problem
- establishing priorities for the agenda
- offering and discussing solutions
- determining steps for implementing solutions
- establishing evaluation and follow-up procedures

Combinations of Information and Action

Purposes of information and action meetings are combined here. In the case of a committee working on a discipline problem it may be necessary for committee members to report the findings of their investigations so that the "next steps" can be formulated and acted upon. Doyle and Strauss (1985, pp. 289–290) offer the following eighteen steps for productive meetings.[1]

Before the Meeting

(1) Plan the meeting carefully: who, what, when, where, why, and how many.
(2) Prepare and send out an agenda in advance.
(3) Come early and set up the meeting room.

At the Beginning of the Meeting

(4) Start on time.
(5) Get participants to introduce themselves and state their expectations for the meeting.
(6) Clearly define roles.
(7) Review, revise, and order the agenda.
(8) Set clear time limits.
(9) Review action items for the previous meeting.

During the Meeting

(10) Focus on the same problem in the same way at the same time.

At the End of the Meeting

(11) Establish action items: who, what, when.
(12) Review the group memory (minutes/notes made on butcher paper).
(13) Set the date and place of the next meeting and develop a preliminary agenda.

---

[1]From *How to Make Meetings Work*. Copyright 1985 by Michael Doyle and David Strauss. Reprinted by permission of the Berkley Publishing Group.

(14) Evaluate the meeting.

(15) Close the meeting crisply and positively.

(16) Clean up and re-arrange the room.

After the Meeting

(17) Prepare the group memo.

(18) Follow up on action items and begin to plan the next meeting.

Principals meet with parents (special interest groups), P.T.A. groups, district-wide teacher or administrator groups, teacher committees from within the school, custodians, aides, bus drivers, student councils, special event committees, etc. The authors too have met with these groups and have found the meetings to be less than productive unless the eighteen steps listed above were followed. It takes a bit more planning time, but the meetings are shorter, there are fewer of them, and we accomplished more.

Guidelines and forms for accomplishing the eighteen steps follow. Identify a meeting coming up at your school and use it as your project for completing the forms provided on the following pages.

Before the Meeting

The agenda provides the leader with a road map to success. It lets participants know in advance the purpose of the meeting and how they can participate. It serves as a guide for the meeting, and it serves as the basis for evaluating the success of the meeting.

Table 7.5 is a sample work form. Like the others, copy it and place it in your file or notebook for future use. Note that Table 7.5 requires identification of the five W's, the type of meeting, and the leader. Ever had trouble determining the intent of a meeting? The authors have, and have conducted a few of them. Use of this planning strategy will help you avoid this problem. Let's start.

What's the name of the group and who will attend? When and where will the group meet? What location? Who will lead the meeting? Provide this information on Table 7.5. Now for the hard part. What is the purpose of the meeting? Be specific. If you can't specify the purpose, the meeting need not be held. If you're stuck, think about what you want from the meeting, the desired out-

TABLE 7.5 **Meeting planning guide: setting up for success.**

WHO	
GROUP/MEETING NAME:	_____
PARTICIPANTS:	_____
	_____
WHERE	
LOCATION:	_____
WHEN	
DATE:	_____
TIME:	_____
WHAT	
1.	_____
2.	_____
3.	_____
4.	_____
5.	_____
PURPOSE (WHY):	_____
MEETING TYPE:	_____
MEETING LEADER:	_____

comes: a decision, list of ideas, a process, etc. If you simply want to present information, the meeting may not be needed. But, if you think there will be questions about the information, your purpose may be to ensure that the group fully understands the information and its implications. In this case, the meeting is needed. If you are facing a rash of discipline problems, the purpose may be to derive a solution to the problem. In this case too the meeting is needed. What is the purpose (desired outcome) of your meeting? Record it on Table 7.5.

Now that the purpose, time, place, and other needed details are decided, it's time to tackle the meat of the agenda. The well-planned agenda includes a statement of the topics to be dealt with, the process to be used in dealing with each topic and the desired product (if any), who will present each topic, and the time allocated to each topic. Each of these must be completed for each topic to ensure the success of the meeting. Use Table 7.6 for planning your meeting.

A detailed agenda works wonders. Here are just a few benefits of a properly planned agenda for both the leader and participants.

Benefits for the Leader

Determines whether the meeting is needed
Serves as a map for accomplishing the results
Ensures that appropriate participants attend
Identifies needed preparation
Keeps the meeting on track
Provides a tool for evaluating success of meeting

TABLE 7.6 **Sample agenda for a successful meeting.**

WHAT:	COUNCIL AGENDA		
WHEN:	NOVEMBER 13, 1987—3:30 P.M.		
WHERE:	CANYON VIEW SCHOOL		

TOPIC:	WHAT:	WHO:	TIME:
Nurse's Home School —Copy Paper & Supplies —Home Schools —Aide Time	Discussion/ Information	Bob	15 min.
Administrators Out of Office —When Out of the District —When Out of the Office	Discussion/ Information	Bob	10 min.
Student Data Base —School System —IBM	Discussion/ Information	Chris	15 min.
Teacher Evaluation Schedule	Discussion/ Est. Sched.	Bob	15 min.
Bus Discipline Procedures	Information/ Est. Dis. Procs.	Gary	10 min.
Time Management	Est. Agenda/ Discussion	Gary	10 min.

Benefits for the Participants

Identifies the topic(s) to be addressed at the meeting and what
   they should study before the meeting
Indicates what to prepare/bring
Communicates what is expected by way of participation

Participants are responsible for studying the agenda and discussions from previous meetings, preparation of new information
needed for the meeting, and formulating ideas for use in the
meeting. The leader should share these expectations with the
participants in a memo or letter which accompanies the agenda.

Expectations for participants during the meeting must also
be communicated. Depending on the purpose of the meeting, participants should play an active role in clarifying purposes, providing information, offering solutions, evaluating solutions,
observing ground rules, clarifying each other's opinions, calling
for a decision, encouraging hesitant participants, asking questions to seek information, making suggestions for keeping the
group on track and protecting the rights of those with minority
opinions.

Be sure the agenda is complete and sent out in advance. Participants should receive it at least two days prior to the meeting and
should be notified of the date, time, and place at least one week in
advance.

Room arrangements sound rather custodial in nature but they
are key to the success of your meeting. Consider the purpose of
your meeting and choose an appropriate room arrangement (see
p. 150). If the purpose is to provide information and conduct some
discussion, plan "A" will work. If it involves problem solving, lots
of discussion and give and take, then plan "B" is appropriate. The
advantage of plan B is that it allows participants to see each
other. This is a very important consideration in problem-solving
meetings. In order to down-play your position as the "boss" during these meetings, don't hold the meeting in your office and don't
sit at the head of the table. Be a participant! Everyone knows
the principal is the boss. The desired effect is for all to participate so that the best possible solution is attained. The image of
"the boss" may restrict the emergence of that much needed solution.

PLAN "A"

Group Memory

Leader

PLAN "B"

Group Memory

Leader

Notice the "Group Memory" in each plan. The group memory is the record of the meeting and is most easily kept on an easel or butcher paper taped to a wall. Keeping the memory is the recorder's job. Information to be recorded varies with the purpose: a decision, list of ideas, a process, questions, etc.

Come to the meeting place early to be sure things are just right. Is the chair and table arrangement correct, are the group memory materials in place, is the temperature comfortable, are paper, pencils, name tags in place, and last, are refreshments appropriate? Everything set? Let's begin the meeting.

Beginning the Meeting

Starting on time may not be popular, but you should do it. The latecomers will either learn to arrive on time or they will drop out. The group may want to establish fines for latecomers. It may help to get people there on time and provide funds for refreshments or the Christmas party. If a significant number of participants are late, the meeting time for the next meeting should be changed. Put it on the next agenda for discussion.

The beginning of the meeting should always be devoted to introductions, where appropriate, and reviewing and gaining consensus on the outcomes and agenda. Are there any comments on the topics? On the purpose and outcome? On the time limits? Should other topics be included? If there is agreement, include it/them. If it will take more time than is available, put it on the next agenda. This may sound like a big time waster, but in the long run it is a time saver. It may take some time to gain consensus but you really can't have a total team effort until you do, and when you do, the force of the team will be much stronger and will help eliminate dissension down the road.

A recorder will be needed and should not be the leader or facilitator. Their time and attention must be free for leading or facilitating. Prerequisites for a good recorder include legible handwriting and the ability to listen to the conversation of the meeting. Caution must be taken to avoid sexism. It's very tempting to choose the female of the group for the job, and this must be avoided at all costs. First, it is not fair, and second, it may cause you a lot of trouble. You may want to call for volunteers or use it as a means to get the non-participator to participate. Determining what should be recorded is also the responsibility of the group, but leadership may be needed. The leader must know what should be recorded before the meeting. The group may offer other helpful ideas.

If the recorder is not sure the true feeling of the group is recorded, he/she should call for clarification. This will ensure accuracy of the memory and facilitate future progress. The memory should be brief. Lengthy minutes cause overload and are difficult to deal with from a historical perspective.

Establishing Ground Rules to Guide the Meeting

Establishing ground rules is another crucial factor. They need not be fancy, but they must be to the point. Some old standbys that really help keep a meeting on track follow:

(1) Let's treat each other with respect. We're in this together and we are not the enemy.
(2) Be honest. If you disagree, it's okay. Say so.
(3) Don't look and listen for fault. Look and listen as an ally, a teammate.
(4) Let's all get our oars in the water and participate, but don't dominate.
(5) Respect the time limits.
(6) One person talks at a time.

These ground rules work wonders. Each is discussed below.

Ground rule 1 is key. We have observed absolutely ridiculous behavior on the part of some people. They are belittling, insulting, ornery, and otherwise just not nice. The inclination is to take them out back and paddle them, but sometimes they are too big and paddling is not an appropriate behavior in a people organization like school, anyway. So, the most we can hope for is adherence to the ground rules, and it works. The bullies may mutter, but there are now rules that give strength to the oppressed to quiet the bullies. Let the ground rules work for you. The participants will use them to do the job. Give it a try.

Disrupters may be people with hidden agendas, i.e. those that do not appear on the formal agenda. Ask them what their point/ agenda is. If they will address it forthrightly, it should go on another agenda if the group agrees. Regardless, it must be addressed or these persons will never be a contributing member of your team.

In summary, gain consensus on the outcomes, purposes, agenda, time limits, contents of the group memory, and ground rules. Have the participants introduce themselves if appropriate, and review the action from the last meeting.

Ground rule 2 helps the timid types participate. Knowing that no one will yell at them or make fun of them (Ground rule 1) may be the encouragement some people need to speak their mind.

Ground rule 3 sets a tone for cooperation. This may take time if there are a lot of skeletons in the closet and a hidden agenda is stuck in someone's craw. Some group building and group processing may be required. But believe us, not much will be accomplished until the skeletons and hidden agendas are dealt with.

Ground rule 4 enhances productivity by encouraging those who typically sit there like a bump on a log grading papers or not paying attention. This may take some one-to-one counseling outside the meeting if the person is particularly shy. Frankly, it is a pretty unusual find in a faculty and is more likely in a P.T.A. group where the participants are not accustomed to speaking in groups. Make them feel relaxed, wanted, and comfortable. The arrangement of the room and chairs, relaxed yet purposeful presentation of topics, and your demeanor will go a long way in helping "bring out" the participants. First and foremost, let them know their participation is valued.

Ground rule 5 keeps the meeting on track. This one also helps limit the verbiage spewed forth by the continual talker. A simple reminder that "we have only five minutes" remaining for this topic will keep them on target.

Ground rule 6 takes care of the person who typically can't keep his/her trap shut. We have all experienced this person. They have something to say about everything and they don't give others an opportunity to speak. Let the ground rules do the work. Remind them of the ground rules which were agreed upon before the meeting. If that doesn't work, the other members of the group will exercise their option of speaking up to control or "shut up" the person in question. Exercise the ground rules. They were agreed upon and people will respect them.

During the Meeting

Follow the agenda and the ground rules—stick to it. If someone brings up a topic they won't drop and it's blocking progress of the meeting, put it in the "bin." That simply means that the recorder notes it in the group memory to be dealt with at another time. It also communicates that the group must continue with the agenda. The recorder should record this on another easel or notebook page for safekeeping. This is the place for the hidden agenda. Get it out in the open so people know what's bothering this person and the person knows the group is listening. Make it clear that the group will deal with the problem at another time. Of course, this should be the group's decision. If the group does not want to deal with it or feels it is not appropriate for the group, deal with it at another time with the person in question. It is mandatory that the topic not cripple the progress of the group's agenda.

At the End of the Meeting

Review the group memory for actions taken and directions established by the group. Remember the who, what, and when format. If assignments were given, make sure the persons responsible know exactly what is expected of them and when it is due. This will help ingrain the decisions in the minds of the participants. Set the time and place of the next meeting. It is much easier and much less time-consuming to do this now than after the group has disbanded.

Evaluate the meeting with the group. A thorough evaluation lets you and the group know what was good about the meeting and what should be changed. Take it seriously; making meetings more effective and efficient is a key to your success. Critiquing meetings for five to ten minutes at the end serves as a reminder of the criteria that contribute to conducting and enjoying good meetings. The important points are to give people an opportunity to voice their opinions about the meeting and to use the information constructively to make the meetings more effective. The number of questions that can be asked are many. A few are provided below for you to select from:

(1) Was the agenda followed?
(2) Did the facilitator remain neutral and effectively facilitate the group?
(3) Did the recorder keep an accurate group memory?
(4) Was the pre-meeting planning adequate?
(5) Were the purposes of the meeting accomplished?
(6) Was there a free flow of ideas and participation?
(7) Was the seating arrangement appropriate?
(8) Were there too many items on the agenda?
(9) Was a win-win solution reached as opposed to a unilateral decision?

(10) Were all participants prepared?

(11) Was the decision already made before the meeting? Was the meeting a rubber stamp?

Administrators spend from 30–70 percent of the work day in meetings. Running better meetings results in greater effectiveness (meaning we get more done better and look good to the boss or board) and it can save a lot of time—time for MBWA.

REFERENCES

ANDREWS, R. L., R. Soder and D. Jacoby. "Principal Roles, Other In-School Variables, and Academic Achievement by Ethnicity and SES." Paper presented at the Annual Meeting of the American Educational Research Association, San Francisco, April 1986.

AQUILA, F. D. "Time Management Tips for School Administrators," *Educ. Digest.*, 54:37–39 (October 1988).

BLAZE, J. J. "Dimensions of Effective School Leadership: The Teacher's Perspective," *America Educational Research Journal*, 24(4):589–610 (1987).

CAWALTI, G. British Columbia Principals Convention, Presentation in Port Albernie, Canada (1987).

DOYLE, M. and D. Straus. *How to Make Meetings Work*. Berkeley, CA:Berkeley Publishing Company, 301 pp. (1985).

DUKE D. L. *School Leadership and Instructional Improvement*. New York:Random House (1987).

GINSBERG, R. "Principals as Instructional Leaders: An Ailing Panacea," *Educ. Urban Soc.*, 20:276–293 (May 1988).

GINSBERG, R. "Worthy Goal . . . Unlikely Reality: The Principal as Instructional Leader," *NASSP Bull.*, 72:76–82 (April 1988).

HAGER, J. L. and L. E. Scarr. "Effective Schools-Effective Principals: How to Develop Both," *Educational Leadership*, 40(5):38–40 (1983).

HARRIS, G. W., Jr. and R. A. Davies. *The Business Management and Service Tasks of the School Principalship.* Springfield, IL:C. C. Thomas (1988).

HOWELL, B. "Profile of the Principalship," *Educational Leadership*, 38:333–336 (Jan. 1981).

HUGHES, L. W. and G. C. Ubben. *The Elementary Principal's Handbook: A Guide to Effective Action*, 3rd edition. Massachusetts:Allyn & Bacon (1989).

KMETZ, J. T. and D. J. Willower. "Elementary School Principals' Work Behavior," *Educational Administration Quarterly*, 18(4):62–78 (1982).

MACKENZIE, R. A. *The Time Trap*. New York:American Management Assn., Inc. (1972).

MARGOLIS, H. and K. J. Tewel. "Resolving Conflict with Parents: A Guide for Administrators," *NASSP Bull.*, 72:1–6+ (March 1988).

MARTIN, W. and D. Willower. "The Managerial Behavior of High School Principals," *Educational Administration Quarterly*, 17(1):69–90 (1981).

MORRIS, V. C., et al. *The Urban Principal: Discretionary Decision-Making in a Large Educational Organization*. Washington, D.C.:National Institute of Education, 239 pp. (ED 207 178) (1981).

MORRIS, V. C., R. L. Crowson, N. C. Nicherson, and J. W. Keefe. *Principals in Action*. Columbus:Charles Merrill (1984).

PALANIUK, S. "How Teachers Get Me into Their Classrooms," *Educ. Leadership*, 46:79 (November 1988).

PARTIN, R. L. "How to Handle Drop-In Visitors," *Principal*, 67:44–45 (March 1988).

PETERSON, K. D. "The Principal's Tasks," *Administrator's Notebook*, 26(8):4 (1977–78).

PIGFORD, A. B. "The Principalship: Five Mistakes I Wish I Had Avoided," *NASSP Bull.*, 72:118–120 (March 1988).

SERGIOVANNI, T. J. and J. H. Moore. *Schooling for Tomorrow: Directing Reform to Issues that Count*. Massachusetts:Allyn & Bacon (1989).

SHIPMAN, N. J., et al. *Effective Time-Management Techniques for School Administrators*. Englewood Cliffs:Prentice-Hall Inc. (1983).

SPROUL, L. "Managerial Attention in New Educational Systems," Seminar on Organizations as Loosely Coupled Systems, Urbana:University of Illinois (Nov. 13–14, 1976).

STRONGE, J. H. "The Elementary School Principalship: A Position in Transition?" *Principal*, 67(5):32–33 (May 1988).

VALENTINE, J., D. Clark, N. Nickerson, and J. Keefe. *The Middle School Principal, 1*. Reston Va:National Association of Secondary School Principals (1981).

WHISENHUNT, D. W. *Administrator Time Management: Tips for Administrators and Aspiring Administrators*. Lanham, MD:University Press of America (1987).

Epilogue

ACCEPTING YOUR FATE OR CREATING YOUR DESTINY: THE CHOICE OF LEADERSHIP

An old Eastern proverb states that man can accept his fate or create his destiny. So can schools. Leadership is a choice between waiting for problems or pursuing goals, between being passive and reactive or being proactive and creative. MBWA is an approach to leadership based on a belief that leadership is visionary, goal-focused, and people-centered. It assumes that improvement on a school, classroom, or personal level is a lifelong journey. It is not an aimless meandering but a purposeful involvement with people to promote school improvement and increased skill development.

MBWA is both diagnostic and prescriptive. Wandering around provides living data of who and what needs strengthening and support. Prescriptively, it is an opportunity to model desired behavior and reinforce people doing things right. MBWA isn't so much an open-door philosophy as a window into the classroom, school, and community. It is leadership that creates opportunity by searching out needs and creating alternatives rather than waiting for problems and hoping for solutions.

MBWA managers know that tomorrow will come, and rather than wait for events to dictate what tomorrow brings, they initiate action to create the future they want. The choice is always yours to make. Children can learn, teachers can teach, and principals can lead, if they choose to.

APPENDIX
A

Twenty-five Steps to Moving from Win-Lose to Win-Win

(1) Recognize that conflict exists.

(2) Realize that building cooperation is difficult.

(3) Accept personal responsibility for resolving the conflict.

(4) Take the initiative to start progress toward cooperation.

(5) Identify "superordinate" goals and work together toward them.

(6) Increase and improve communication.

(7) Identify and overcome barriers to effective communication.

(8) Strive to understand one another's point of view.

(9) Listen to the other's point of view.

(10) Expect to be listened to.

(11) Attempt to build openness and trust.

(12) Attempt to stay rational and avoid being emotional.

(13) Never throw the first stone.

(14) Avoid the urge to retaliate.

(15) Take one step at a time together, not quantum leaps.

(16) Be willing to take reasonable risks together.

(17) Avoid "absolute" positions.

(18) Be willing to compromise.

(19) Strive for complete honesty.

(20) Keep your word and expect the same.

(21) Be willing to admit your mistakes.

(22) Replace old, negative patterns with new, positive ones.

(23) Reiterate the advantages of cooperation and the dangers of competition.

(24) Recognize and reward cooperative effort.

(25) Remember, two winners are better than one.

BEHAVIORAL CHARACTERISTICS OF WIN-LOSE VS. WIN-WIN GROUPS

Win-Lose Competition	Win-Win Cooperation
Closed Communication	Open Communication
Distrust and Suspicion	Mutual Trust
Dishonesty and Deception	Honesty and Candor
Intolerance and Insensitivity	Tolerance and Sensitivity
Emotional, Defensive, and Hostile	Rational and Calm
No Desire to Understand Other's Point of View	Strong Desire to Understand Other's Point of View
Short Time Perspective	Long Time Perspective
Personal Goal Orientation	Joint Goal Orientation
Determined to "Get Own Way"	Determined to Resolve Conflict Together
Must be a "Winner" and "Loser"	Can Both Be "Winners"
Loyalty before Logic	Logic before Loyalty
Strong Desire to Retaliate	Turn Other Cheek
Personal Attacks against "Opponent"	Build Interpersonal Relations
Protective of Own Resources	Willing to Share Resources
No Compromise Seen as Possible	Mutually Acceptable Solution Seen as Possible

Elementary School Parent Survey

SEVERAL areas of interest have been identified in the questionnaire below. We would like to have an indication of your feelings about these areas and the importance you attach to them. In the center of the page is a series of statements. Please indicate your agreement or disagreement that each statement is true of _____ School *now* by marking the scale to the left. On the right of each statement, please indicate the importance you attach to it. Each statement should have two responses. Space has been provided for your comments and suggestions below each section.

Please circle the grade(s) that your child/children attend.

K   1   2   3   4   5   6

A Strongly agree
B Agree
C Disagree
D Strongly Disagree
E Lack Info to Respond

1 Very Important
2 Important
3 Somewhat Important
4 Not Important

DO I AGREE OR DISAGREE WITH THIS STATEMENT?

HOW IMPORTANT IS THIS AREA TO ME?

COMMUNICATION:

A B C D E 1. The school communicates clearly its rules and standards of behavior to parents.   **1 2 3 4**

A B C D E 2. The school keeps parents informed of school activities.   **1 2 3 4**

161

DO I AGREE OR DISAGREE   **HOW IMPORTANT IS THIS**
WITH THIS STATEMENT?   **AREA TO ME?**

COMMUNICATION:

A B C D E 3. Students have the opportunity to   **1   2   3   4**
communicate their interests and con-
cerns to teachers.

A B C D E 4. Students are kept informed of their   **1   2   3   4**
progress by teachers.

A B C D E 5. Parents are encouraged to discuss   **1   2   3   4**
their children's problems with
teachers.

6. The following types of communication
between home and school work well
to keep parents informed:

A B C D E   a) What-to-Expect-Night   **1   2   3   4**
A B C D E   b) Teacher Notes and Phone Calls   **1   2   3   4**
A B C D E   c) Report Cards   **1   2   3   4**
A B C D E   d) Parent–Teacher Conference   **1   2   3   4**
A B C D E   e) Open House   **1   2   3   4**
A B C D E   f) The Thursday Bulletin   **1   2   3   4**

Comments: _____
_____
_____
_____
_____

DO I AGREE OR DISAGREE   **HOW IMPORTANT IS THIS**
WITH THIS STATEMENT?   **AREA TO ME?**

STUDENT BEHAVIOR:

A B C D E 1. Students in our school are generally   **1   2   3   4**
respectful of each other.

A B C D E 2. Most students and teachers in our   **1   2   3   4**
school maintain good working rela-
tionships.

A B C D E 3. Our school is doing a good job of   **1   2   3   4**
helping my child understand his/her
responsibilities as a student.

A B C D E 4. Our school helps my child to under-   **1   2   3   4**

| **DO I AGREE OR DISAGREE WITH THIS STATEMENT?** | | | | | | **HOW IMPORTANT IS THIS AREA TO ME?** | | | |

STUDENT BEHAVIOR:

stand and get along with other people.

A	B	C	D	E	5. Discipline is not a serious problem in our school.	1 2 3 4
A	B	C	D	E	6. Our school places appropriate emphasis on the social development of my child.	1 2 3 4
A	B	C	D	E	7. My child looks forward to school each day.	1 2 3 4
A	B	C	D	E	8. The overall morale of students in our school is good.	1 2 3 4
A	B	C	D	E	9. School rules and regulations affecting my child are reasonable.	1 2 3 4

Comments: _____
_____
_____
_____
_____

DO I AGREE OR DISAGREE WITH THIS STATEMENT?   **HOW IMPORTANT IS THIS AREA TO ME?**

CURRICULUM:

1. The following curricular areas are meeting our students' needs:

A	B	C	D	E	a) Spelling	1 2 3 4
A	B	C	D	E	b) Grammar	1 2 3 4
A	B	C	D	E	c) Written Composition	1 2 3 4
A	B	C	D	E	d) Creative Writing	1 2 3 4
A	B	C	D	E	e) Reading	1 2 3 4
A	B	C	D	E	f) Social Studies	1 2 3 4
A	B	C	D	E	g) Science	1 2 3 4
A	B	C	D	E	h) Mathematics	1 2 3 4
A	B	C	D	E	i) Foreign Language	1 2 3 4
A	B	C	D	E	j) Physical Education	1 2 3 4
A	B	C	D	E	k) Music	1 2 3 4

DO I AGREE OR DISAGREE   **HOW IMPORTANT IS THIS**
WITH THIS STATEMENT?   **AREA TO ME?**

CURRICULUM:

A	B	C	D	E	l) Art	1	2	3	4
A	B	C	D	E	m) Library	1	2	3	4
A	B	C	D	E	n) Computer	1	2	3	4

2. Students with special needs are receiving appropriate services in the following areas:

A	B	C	D	E	a) Health	1	2	3	4
A	B	C	D	E	b) Counseling	1	2	3	4
A	B	C	D	E	c) Resource/Learning Problems	1	2	3	4
A	B	C	D	E	d) Speech and Language	1	2	3	4
A	B	C	D	E	e) Challenge/Gifted	1	2	3	4
A	B	C	D	E	3. Children have adequate equipment, materials, and supplies available at school.	1	2	3	4

4. The school devotes appropriate time to cultural enrichment through:

A	B	C	D	E	a) Assemblies	1	2	3	4
A	B	C	D	E	b) Field Trips	1	2	3	4

Comments: _____
_____
_____
_____
_____

DO I AGREE OR DISAGREE   **HOW IMPORTANT IS THIS**
WITH THIS STATEMENT?   **AREA TO ME?**

TEACHERS AND INSTRUCTION:

A	B	C	D	E	1. Teachers in our school are concerned about my child as an individual.	1	2	3	4
A	B	C	D	E	2. Our teachers appropriately emphasize developing critical thinking skills, i.e., problem solving, estimating, analyzing, etc.	1	2	3	4

DO I AGREE OR DISAGREE WITH THIS STATEMENT?	HOW IMPORTANT IS THIS AREA TO ME?

TEACHERS AND INSTRUCTION:

A B C D E 3. Our teachers are competent.   **1 2 3 4**

A B C D E 4. Our school provides my child with opportunities to reach full potential.   **1 2 3 4**

A B C D E 5. Our school places proper emphasis on grading.   **1 2 3 4**

A B C D E 6. Our school pursues innovative instructional methods.   **1 2 3 4**

A B C D E 7. It is easy to make appointments to see teachers in our school.   **1 2 3 4**

A B C D E 8. My child receives the personal attention needed in the classroom from his/her teachers.   **1 2 3 4**

A B C D E 9. Homework assignments are meaningful.   **1 2 3 4**

10. The amount of homework is:

A B C D E   a) Too much   **1 2 3 4**

A B C D E   b) Too little   **1 2 3 4**

A B C D E   c) Enough   **1 2 3 4**

A B C D E 11. Teachers utilize a variety of methods to teach students.   **1 2 3 4**

Comments: _____
_____
_____
_____
_____

DO I AGREE OR DISAGREE WITH THIS STATEMENT?	HOW IMPORTANT IS THIS AREA TO ME?

ADMINISTRATION:

1. Class size is:

A B C D E   a) Too large   **1 2 3 4**

A B C D E   b) Too small   **1 2 3 4**

A B C D E   c) About right   **1 2 3 4**

A B C D E 2. Custodial service is adequate.   **1 2 3 4**

DO I AGREE OR DISAGREE   **HOW IMPORTANT IS THIS**
WITH THIS STATEMENT?   **AREA TO ME?**

ADMINISTRATION:

3. The school is well-maintained with
regard to:

A B C D E   a) Buildings   1 2 3 4
A B C D E   b) Grounds   1 2 3 4
A B C D E   c) Equipment   1 2 3 4
A B C D E 4. The present bus service meets   1 2 3 4
the needs of students.
A B C D E 5. The principal continually strives to   1 2 3 4
improve the effectiveness of our
school.
A B C D E 6. The principal is available   1 2 3 4
to listen to parent concerns.
A B C D E 7. The principal is visible.   1 2 3 4
A B C D E 8. The principal is positively   1 2 3 4
perceived by children.
A B C D E 9. The FFA is an effective   1 2 3 4
parent organization.

Comments: _____
_____
_____
_____
_____

Junior High Parent Survey

1. Students in our school are generally respectful of each other.
    A. Strongly Agree
    B. Agree
    C. Don't Know
    D. Disagree
    E. Strongly Disagree

2. Most students and teachers in our school maintain good working relationships.
    A. Strongly Agree
    B. Agree
    C. Don't Know
    D. Disagree
    E. Strongly Disagree

3. Substance abuse in our school is not a serious problem.
    A. Strongly Agree
    B. Agree
    C. Don't Know
    D. Disagree
    E. Strongly Disagree

4. Decisions made by our school reflect the concerns of parents.
    A. Strongly Agree
    B. Agree
    C. Don't Know
    D. Disagree
    E. Strongly Disagree

5. Our school is doing a good job of helping my child understand his/her responsibilities as a student.
   A. Strongly Agree
   B. Agree
   C. Don't Know
   D. Disagree
   E. Strongly Disagree

6. Teachers in our school are concerned about my child as an individual.
   A. Strongly Agree
   B. Agree
   C. Don't Know
   D. Disagree
   E. Strongly Disagree

7. Our school helps my child to understand and get along with other people.
   A. Strongly Agree
   B. Agree
   C. Don't Know
   D. Disagree
   E. Strongly Disagree

8. Discipline is not a serious problem in our school.
   A. Strongly Agree
   B. Agree
   C. Don't Know
   D. Disagree
   E. Strongly Disagree

9. Reports from our school concerning my child's progress are helpful.
   A. Strongly Agree
   B. Agree
   C. Don't Know
   D. Disagree
   E. Strongly Disagree

10. Theft is not a serious problem in our school.
   A. Strongly Agree
   B. Agree
   C. Don't Know
   D. Disagree
   E. Strongly Disagree

11. Our school places appropriate emphasis on the social development of my child.
   A. Strongly Agree
   B. Agree

C. Don't Know
D. Disagree
E. Strongly Disagree

12. Our school's physical plant is well-maintained.

A. Strongly Agree
B. Agree
C. Don't Know
D. Disagree
E. Strongly Disagree

13. Our teachers appropriately emphasize developing critical thinking skills, i.e., problem solving, analyzing.

A. Strongly Agree
B. Agree
C. Don't Know
D. Disagree
E. Strongly Disagree

14. Our teachers are competent.

A. Strongly Agree
B. Agree
C. Don't Know
D. Disagree
E. Strongly Disagree

15. Our school provides my child with opportunities to reach full potential.

A. Strongly Agree
B. Agree
C. Don't Know
D. Disagree
E. Strongly Disagree

16. Cheating is not a serious problem in our school.

A. Strongly Agree
B. Agree
C. Don't Know
D. Disagree
E. Strongly Disagree

17. Our school places proper emphasis on grading.

A. Strongly Agree
B. Agree
C. Don't Know
D. Disagree
E. Strongly Disagree

18. Our school pursues innovative instructional methods.

A. Strongly Agree

B. Agree
C. Don't Know
D. Disagree
E. Strongly Disagree

19. Our school's extracurricular activities program is sufficient to meet the needs of my child.
    A. Strongly Agree
    B. Agree
    C. Don't Know
    D. Disagree
    E. Strongly Disagree

20. Student participation in extracurricular activities is an important aspect of education at our school.
    A. Strongly Agree
    B. Agree
    C. Don't Know
    D. Disagree
    E. Strongly Disagree

21. The services provided by our school's counselor are supportive of my child's present needs.
    A. Strongly Agree
    B. Agree
    C. Don't Know
    D. Disagree
    E. Strongly Disagree

22. Our school's health services are adequate.
    A. Strongly Agree
    B. Agree
    C. Don't Know
    D. Disagree
    E. Strongly Disagree

23. Transportation services provided by our school meet my child's needs.
    A. Strongly Agree
    B. Agree
    C. Don't Know
    D. Disagree
    E. Strongly Disagree

24. Vandalism is not a serious problem at our school.
    A. Strongly Agree
    B. Agree
    C. Don't Know
    D. Disagree
    E. Strongly Disagree

25. My child looks forward to going to school each day.
   A. Strongly Agree
   B. Agree
   C. Don't Know
   D. Disagree
   E. Strongly Disagree

26. The overall morale of students in our school is good.
   A. Strongly Agree
   B. Agree
   C. Don't Know
   D. Disagree
   E. Strongly Disagree

27. It is easy to make appointments to see teachers in our school.
   A. Strongly Agree
   B. Agree
   C. Don't Know
   D. Disagree
   E. Strongly Disagree

28. The principal continually strives to improve the effectiveness of our school.
   A. Strongly Agree
   B. Agree
   C. Don't Know
   D. Disagree
   E. Strongly Disagree

29. The principal is available to listen to parent concerns.
   A. Strongly Agree
   B. Agree
   C. Don't Know
   D. Disagree
   E. Strongly Disagree

30. My child receives the personal attention needed in the classroom from his/her teachers.
   A. Strongly Agree
   B. Agree
   C. Don't Know
   D. Disagree
   E. Strongly Disagree

31. School rules and regulations affecting my child are reasonable.
   A. Strongly Agree
   B. Agree
   C. Don't Know
   D. Disagree
   E. Strongly Disagree

32. The electives offered at our school are sufficient to meet the needs of my child.
   A.   Strongly Agree
   B.   Agree
   C.   Don't Know
   D.   Disagree
   E.   Strongly Disagree

33. In what grades do you have children at the junior high?
   ☐   7th Grade
   ☐   8th Grade
   ☐   Both 7th and 8th Grade

34. Rate the quality of each of the following programs at our school:

	poor	fair	average	good	excellent	don't know
Art						
Music						
P.E.						
Reading						
Math						
Science						
Social Studies						
English						
Foreign Languages						
Drama						
Counseling						
Resource Room						

APPENDIX
D

Catalina Foothills School District
Summative Evaluation Report
Teacher Performance Evaluation

Teacher's Name _____ Date _____ Grade/Subject _____

PERFORMANCE AREA I: EFFECTIVE LESSON PLANNING

CRITERIA	LEVELS OF PERFORMANCE		
A. Demonstrates effective instructional planning skills.	___ Inadequate	___ Targeted for Improvement	___ Professionally Proficient
___ Not Observed	Does not demonstrate evidence of effective planning.	Needs to improve how the evidence of planning is demonstrated.	Demonstrates evidence of effective planning.
Comments:			
B. Selects appropriate objectives.	___ Inadequate	___ Targeted for Improvement	___ Professionally Proficient
___ Not Observed	Does not select appropriate objectives.	Needs to select appropriate objectives more consistently.	Consistently selects objectives that are appropriate for the topic and students.
Comments:			
C. Assesses student learning.	___ Inadequate	___ Targeted for Improvement	___ Professionally Proficient
___ Not Observed	Does not assess student learning.	Needs to improve upon assessing student learning.	Systematically assesses student learning and uses the data for instructional planning.
Comments:			

PERFORMANCE AREA II: EFFECTIVE CLASSROOM MANAGEMENT

CRITERIA	LEVELS OF PERFORMANCE		

A. Establishes and reinforces high standards for student discipline.

___ Not Observed
Comments:

___ Inadequate	___ Targeted for Improvement	___ Professionally Proficient
Does not establish/ reinforce high standards for student discipline.	Needs to improve how standards for student discipline are established/reinforced.	Establishes and reinforces high standards for student discipline in the classroom.

B. Maximizes student time on task.

___ Not Observed
Comments:

___ Inadequate	___ Targeted for Improvement	___ Professionally Proficient
Does not use techniques that maximize student time on task.	Needs to improve in using techniques that maximize student time on task.	Uses techniques that maximize student time on task.

PERFORMANCE AREA III: EFFECTIVE TEACHING PRACTICES

CRITERIA	LEVELS OF PERFORMANCE		

A. Teaches to the objective.

___ Not Observed
Comments:

___ Inadequate	___ Targeted for Improvement	___ Professionally Proficient
Does not teach to objective.	Needs to improve upon teaching to the objective.	Teacher actions are congruent with the objective.

B. Monitors and adjusts instruction.

___ Not Observed
Comments:

___ Inadequate	___ Targeted for Improvement	___ Professionally Proficient
Does not monitor and adjust instruction.	Needs to improve upon monitoring and adjusting instruction.	Consistently monitors and adjusts instruction.

C. Communicates and reinforces high expectations for student achievement.	___ Inadequate	___ Targeted for Improvement	___ Professionally Proficient
___ Not Observed Comments:	Does not communicate and reinforce high expectations for student achievement.	Needs to improve upon communicating and reinforcing high expectations for student achievement.	Consistently communicates and reinforces high expectations for student achievement.

D. Demonstrates the ability to motivate students.	___ Inadequate	___ Targeted for Improvement	___ Professionally Proficient
___ Not Observed Comments:	Does not demonstrate ability to motivate students.	Needs to improve ability to motivate students.	Demonstrates ability to motivate students.

E. Effectively reinforces learning through the use of appropriate practice.	___ Inadequate	___ Targeted for Improvement	___ Professionally Proficient
___ Not Observed Comments:	Does not effectively reinforce learning through appropriate practice.	Needs to improve effective reinforcement of learning through appropriate practice.	Effectively reinforces learning through the use of appropriate practice.

F. Demonstrates effective lesson presentation skills.	___ Inadequate	___ Targeted for Improvement	___ Professionally Proficient
___ Not Observed Comments:	Does not demonstrate effective lesson presentation skills.	Needs to improve lesson presentation skills.	Uses effective lesson presentation skills.

PERFORMANCE AREA IV: POSITIVE INTERPERSONAL RELATIONS

CRITERIA	LEVELS OF PERFORMANCE		
A. Demonstrates effective inter-personal relations with parents. ___ Not Observed Comments:	___ Inadequate Does not demon-strate effective interpersonal re-lations with parents.	___ Targeted for Improvement Needs to improve interpersonal rela-tions with parents.	___ Professionally Proficient Demonstrates effec-tive interpersonal relations with parents.
B. Demonstrates effective inter-personal relations with colleagues, administrators, and other support personnel. ___ Not Observed Comments:	___ Inadequate Does not demon-strate effective interpersonal re-lations with colleagues, administrators, and other support personnel.	___ Targeted for Improvement Needs to improve interpersonal rela-tions with col-leagues, adminis-trators, and other support personnel.	___ Professionally Proficient Demonstrates effec-tive interpersonal relations with colleagues, admin-istrators, and other support personnel.
C. Demonstrates interpersonal skills in relating to students. ___ Not Observed Comments:	___ Inadequate Does not demon-strate interper-sonal skills in relating to students.	___ Targeted for Improvement Needs to improve interpersonal skills in relating to students.	___ Professionally Proficient Demonstrates effec-tive interpersonal skills in relating to students.

| D. Actively uses techniques to build positive student self-esteem.

___ Not Observed
Comments: | ___ Inadequate

Does not use techniques to build positive student self-esteem. | ___ Targeted for Improvement

Inconsistently uses techniques which build positive student self-esteem. | ___ Professionally Proficient

Actively uses techniques to build positive student self-esteem. |

PERFORMANCE AREA V: PROFESSIONAL RESPONSIBILITY

CRITERIA	LEVELS OF PERFORMANCE		
A. Demonstrates employee responsibility. ___ Not Observed Comments:	___ Inadequate Does not demonstrate employee responsibility.	___ Targeted for Improvement Needs to consistently demonstrate employee responsibility.	___ Professionally Proficient Demonstrates employee responsibility.
B. Pursues professional growth. ___ Not Observed Comments:	___ Inadequate Does not pursue professional growth.	___ Targeted for Improvement Needs to improve upon how professional growth is pursued.	___ Professionally Proficient Pursues professional growth.

TEACHER EVALUATION TIMELINE
Planning Conference   _____

Formal Observations   observation   _____

                                       post-conference   _____

observation   _____

post-conference   _____

Other Observations   _____

Summative Conference   _____

Professional Growth Plan Due   _____

Signature indicates that the teacher and evaluator have reviewed and discussed the evaluation report. (A summary statement from either the teacher or evaluator is optional.)

Teacher's Signature _____   Date _____

Evaluator's Signature _____   Date _____

OPTIONAL COMMENTS:

WHITE COPY—PERSONNEL
YELLOW COPY—EVALUATOR
PINK COPY—TEACHER

APPENDIX E

Teacher Self-Assessment Inventory of Skills and Interests

INTERPERSONAL COMMUNICATION

1. Learning strategies for communicating to the community.
2. Communicating and interacting with parents.
3. Knowing when and where to refer student problems.
4. Developing strategies to successfully involve classroom assistants.
5. Initiating and building professional relationships with colleagues.
6. Resolving teacher/administrator differences in a positive and effective manner.
7. Other.

DEVELOPING PUPIL SELF-ESTEEM

8. Facilitating pupil self-concept and worth.
9. Facilitating pupil social interaction.
10. Instilling in the student the will to learn on his own initiative.
11. Other.

INDIVIDUALIZING INSTRUCTION

12. Assessing and selecting appropriate materials and activities for individualized instruction.
13. Creating and developing materials and learning options.
14. Implementing and supervising individualized instruction.
15. Other.

ASSESSMENT

16. Coping with the task of evaluating and communicating student progress.
17. Selecting and specifying performance goals and objectives.
18. Establishing appropriate performance standards.
19. Constructing and using tests for evaluating academic progress.
20. Involving students in self-evaluation.
21. Diagnosing basic learning difficulties.
22. Identifying students with disabilities who need referral or special remedial work.
23. Other.

DISCIPLINE

24. Using methods of classroom discipline at appropriate times.
25. Maintaining classroom control without appearing as an ogre to students.
26. Identifying student attitudes as an aid to solving problems in and out of the classroom.
27. Other.

DEVELOPING PERSONAL AND PROFESSIONAL HELP

28. Evaluating your instructional methods and procedures.
29. Developing or modifying instructional procedures to suit your own strengths.
30. Developing a personal self-evaluation method.
31. Developing a greater capacity for accepting other's feelings.
32. Other.

ORGANIZING FOR INSTRUCTION

33. Using alternative methods in school organization—multi-age grouping, continuous progress, open classroom, minicourses.
34. Utilizing staff resources—team teaching, aides, flexible scheduling.
35. Deciding on appropriate pupil grouping procedures for instruction within the classroom.
36. Creating optimum physical environment for learning.
37. Managing classrooms in order to get maximum learning.
38. Presenting information and directions.
39. Deciding which teaching technique is best suited for a specific purpose.

40. Using questioning procedures that facilitate learning.
41. Gearing instruction to problem solving.
42. Using multimedia.
43. Providing for reinforcement of basic skills.
44. Other.

FUTURE TRENDS AND ISSUES IN EDUCATION

45. Keeping abreast of developments in your own subject matter area.
46. Year-round schools.
47. Mainstreaming disabled children.
48. Alternative education programs.
49. Vocational and career education.
50. Teacher centers.
51. Professional retraining for future manpower needs.
52. Legislation affecting teachers.
53. Other.

APPENDIX F

Catalina Foothills School District, Tucson, Arizona, Teacher Evaluation Performance Areas, Criteria, and Indicators

INDICATORS are examples and guides in defining criteria. Those with an asterisk are considered essential to professional proficiency.

I. Effective Lesson Planning

A. Demonstrates Effective Instructional Planning Skills
*1. Uses instructional objectives congruent with district curriculum.
*2. Can write or verbalize learning behavior for the intended objective.
*3. Selects topics and activities congruent with instructional objective.
*4. Plans instruction to accommodate varying levels of ability.
*5. Writes daily lesson plans in a form comprehensible to substitutes or administrators.
6. Plans formative and summative evaluation procedures.
*7. Has developed and follows course or unit outlines for prescribed curricula.
8. Assists students in defining realistic self-development goals.
9. Can write a five-step lesson plan.
10. Plans for use of high interest media and activities.
11. Plans instruction to accommodate varying learning styles.
12. Plans for development of critical thinking, including objectives at all levels of Bloom's Taxonomy: knowledge, comprehension, application, analysis, synthesis, and evaluation.

B. Selects Appropriate Objectives
*1. Selects objectives at correct levels of difficulty for all students.
*2. Chooses materials and instructional methods appropriate to students' abilities and interests.
*3. Selects accurate and up-to-date information for lessons.
*4. Adjusts objectives for special needs students.

     5. Utilizes task analysis in developing lesson plans.

     6. Incorporates lesson objectives from all levels of Bloom's Taxonomy.

C. **Assesses Student Learning**

  *1. Has and uses a plan for assessing student learning.

  *2. Utilizes reliable and valid assessment instruments and procedures.

  *3. Systematically collects assessment data.

  *4. Uses assessment data for program evaluation and modification.

  *5. Can provide evidence of student progress.

  *6. Maintains written records of pertinent progress data for all students.

   7. Can describe strengths and weaknesses of instructional program.

   8. Uses results of student standardized test data to assess learning.

   9. Discusses graded work with individual students and small groups, assuring their recognition of ways of improving performance or overcoming difficulties.

  10. Shares diagnostic data with individual students, helping them to set specific, realistic learning objectives.

  11. Has and uses a plan to assess student attitudes.

II. **Effective Classroom Management**

A. **Establishes and Reinforces High Standards for Student Discipline**

  *1. Manages discipline in accordance with school procedures, school board policies, and legal requirements.

  *2. Defines limits of acceptable behavior, consequences of misbehavior, and communicates these to students and their parents.

  *3. Attends to disruptions quickly and firmly.

  *4. Demonstrates fairness and consistency in handling student problems, always maintaining the dignity of individuals.

  *5. Uses a behavior management system based on sound psychological theory and research.

  *6. Uses a discipline plan based on the encouragement and recognition of positive, appropriate student behavior.

   7. Uses voice control, cues, hand signals, eye contact and/or other techniques to establish desired behavior.

   8. Uses procedures and practices to promote self-discipline.

   9. Teaches students appropriate behaviors and has students rehearse them.

  10. Posts classroom rules.

  11. Has a plan for dealing with potential major problems.

B. Maximizes Student Time on Task
*1. Schedules learning time in accordance with district policy.
*2. Maintains a purposeful and orderly but not rigid classroom climate.
*3. Establishes procedures so students know what to do upon completing a task or when needing help.
*4. Efficiently manages time by starting class and lessons promptly and closing lessons smoothly within allotted time.
*5. Ensures students are engaged in task relevant activities.
*6. Ensures students experience a high rate of task success.
*7. Ensures a high percentage of students are on task at all times.
*8. Minimizes time spent in collecting or disseminating materials and in making transitions between subjects, classes, or activities.

III. Effective Teaching Practices
A. Teaches to the Objective
*1. Uses models, explanations, information, questions, activities, and responses that are congruent with objectives.
*2. Reinforces student responses congruent with objectives.
*3. Provides practice congruent with objectives.
4. Refrains from losing the objective focus through digression or irrelevant information.

B. Monitors and Adjusts Instruction
*1. Elicits appropriate overt behavior from the whole group or individuals to monitor understanding.
*2. Reteaches, elaborates, or alters instruction based on having monitored student behavior.
*3. Alters the pace of instruction based on monitoring.
4. Circulates and observes behavior to monitor level of understanding.
5. Provides alternative activities for special needs students.
6. Uses formative evaluation techniques for monitoring.

C. Communicates and Reinforces High Expectations for Student Achievement
*1. Bases expectations on observed student needs and potential.
*2. Provides encouragement and response opportunities for all students.
*3. Uses techniques such as latency, delving, praise, and proximity control to ensure equitable response opportunities.
*4. Projects an attitude that all students can learn.
*5. Maintains clear, firm, and reasonable work standards and due dates.

6. Promotes personal goal setting through use of contracts and conferences, as appropriate.
7. Provides gifted and high achieving students with higher level work rather than a greater quantity.
8. Takes time to write supportive comments on report cards, homework, and classroom work.

D. **Demonstrates the Ability to Motivate Students**
   *1. Expresses genuine interest, enthusiasm, and curiosity about subject matter and activities.
   2. Utilizes novelty, vividness, and relevancy to interest students.
   *3. Provides specific and immediate feedback to motivate students.
   *4. Strives for success by providing support, encouragement, appropriate tasks, and corrective feedback.
   *5. Utilizes a variety of active participation strategies.
   6. Communicates excitement about the lesson with facial expressions, voice inflections, gestures, and movement.
   7. Exhibits a high degree of energy and vitality.
   8. Invests time to decorate and arrange an interesting room that reinforces instructional goals.
   9. Involves students actively and regularly in such multisensory experiences as dramatizations, games, media, presentations, field trips, simulations, and labs.
   10. Increases and decreases the level of concern to keep students motivated.
   11. Utilizes pleasant and unpleasant feeling tone to motivate students.

E. **Effectively Reinforces Learning through the Use of Appropriate Practice**
   *1. Prepares students to perform assignments independently and at a high success rate.
   *2. Introduces new concepts and vocabulary found in assignments.
   *3. Provides feedback on assignments within a reasonable amount of time.
   4. Communicates specific purpose of the assignment.
   *5. Follows school and/or district homework guidelines.
   *6. Provides many short and intense practice periods or mass practice at the beginning of learning and then distributes practice periods over time to insure retention.
   7. Maintains a schedule for the intermittent review of key concepts or skills.

F. **Demonstrates Effective Lesson Presentation Skills**
   *1. Presents ideas sequentially and clearly.
   *2. Gives easily understood directions.

*3. Checks for understanding and repeats or rephrases as necessary.

*4. Provides feedback on correctness or incorrectness of classroom work.

*5. Adjusts pace of questioning to allow appropriate wait time.

*6. Uses an array of question types, ranging from simple recognition and recall to interpretive, open-ended and evaluative.

*7. Elicits a deliberate focus and mental readiness to prepare students for lessons.

*8. Reviews previously learned concepts or skills that are essential prerequisites to new learning.

*9. Leads students to summarize the main points of lessons through discussion, activities, and/or questions.

10. Posts or writes important information on the board.

IV. Positive Interpersonal Relations

A. Demonstrates Effective Interpersonal Relations

*1. Uses data, work samples, and anecdotal records in conferences.

*2. Refrains from exhibiting defensiveness, hostility, or anger in conferences.

*3. Initiates parent contacts for students with problems.

4. Uses active listening techniques such as paraphrasing.

5. Provides written expectations for homework and discipline.

6. Provides parents with a written or oral overview of instructional programs.

7. Initiates a system for reporting positive student behavior or achievement such as awards and happy-grams.

B. Demonstrates Effective Interpersonal Relations with Colleagues, Administrators, and Other Support Personnel

*1. Refrains from criticizing, chastising, or belittling other employees.

*2. Treats other employees respectfully and courteously.

*3. Deals with personal and professional concerns in a direct, confidential and appropriate manner.

*4. Cooperates with support personnel.

*5. Avoids undermining committees and group efforts in planning and problem solving.

6. Shares ideas, materials, and methods with colleagues.

7. Maintains an optimistic and positive attitude in dealings with others.

C. Demonstrates Interpersonal Skills in Relating to Students

*1. Makes time available for students who need to see the teacher.

*2. Uses discretion in handling confidential information.

*3. Demonstrates patience and interest when speaking with students.

*4. Discusses student behavior in terms of problem solving as to how to help students grow and improve.

*5. Demonstrates a respect and concern for student welfare.

6. Acknowledges and respects the rights of students to hold differing views or values.

7. Can discuss each student's interests, background, and general personality.

8. Uses names of students in a warm and friendly way when addressing them.

9. Uses with and accepts from students, such physical contacts as handshakes, pats on the back, or hugs.

10. Uses active listening skills with students such as parroting, paraphrasing, and body language.

D. **Actively Uses Techniques to Build Positive Student Self-Esteem**

*1. Provides opportunities for all students to achieve recognition for constructive behavior and academic progress.

*2. Provides opportunities for all students to regularly meet academic success.

*3. Provides positive, constructive feedback and avoids sarcasm and belittling.

*4. Refrains from exhibiting hostility, shouting, or excessive anger.

5. Shows a sensitivity to the physical, emotional, and social needs of students by providing verbal support, encouragement, and exhibiting patience.

6. Has students monitor their own progress.

7. Reinforces student self-control with praise and encouragement.

V. **Professional Responsibility**

A. **Demonstrates Employee Responsibility**

*1. Responds appropriately to parental concern.

2. Provides accurate, timely data as requested by the principal or district administration.

*3. Maintains teaching tools and equipment in good condition.

*4. Demonstrates responsibility for student behavior throughout the entire school.

*5. Models appropriate behavior at school functions such as assemblies and concerts.

*6. Adheres to authorized school and district policies.

*7. Utilizes appropriate channels for resolving concerns.

8. Stays informed of policies and procedures.

9. Participates in the total realm of school activities.

10. Avoids undermining official committee and faculty decisions.

11. Demonstrates a positive and constructive attitude.

B. **Pursues Professional Growth**

  *1. Selects growth activities relevant to district-adopted performance areas and criteria.

  *2. Engages in self-assessment activities that lead toward selection of growth activities.

  *3. Stays informed of current professional practices, research, and content.

  *4. Demonstrates an openness to professional improvement, growth, and supervisory feedback.

   5. Provides a rationale for growth activities, as requested.

   6. Balances release time activities with classroom responsibilities.

Disciplinary Procedures

CANYON View School has set guidelines to ensure consistency in discipline on school premises. We want parents to know that school rules are designed to protect all children. Students who break rules are treated firmly, kindly, and appropriately from day to day and from student to student.

Most students never have serious discipline problems. To protect rights of all our children, it's important that parents and students understand the consequences of misbehavior. While each situation is assessed individually, generally the following sequence will occur.

CLASSROOM PROBLEMS

STEP ONE

Class Behavior System: Each teacher will tell, explain, practice, and post class rules, consequences, and rewards.

STEP TWO

Informal Talk: The teacher will informally talk with the student to work out a plan of action to avoid the problem in the future.

STEP THREE

Specific behavior plan developed tailored to identify individual goals, rewards, and consequences.

189

SCHOOLWIDE, OUTSIDE THE CLASSROOM PROBLEMS

STEP ONE

School rules and consequences established, taught to all students, practiced, and reinforced.

STEP TWO

Quiet Room: School adults will follow the procedures established by the staff if students break school rules. Reasons for a Quiet Room referral are: continued violation of school rules after one warning for the same violation has been issued. In addition, the following violations earn an immediate referral to the Quiet Room: fighting, blatant noncompliance with school rules or adult requests, blatant arguing, and endangering self or others.

STEP THREE

For students exhibiting a chronic pattern of school-wide misbehavior or an acute incident the following will take place.

Parent Conference: A conference with the teacher, principal, and parent may be held to formulate a behavior change plan.

Privilege Suspension: The principal may notify the parent and student of privilege suspension. These privileges include bus, playground, MPR, computer lab, library, or participation in class or school special events.

Severe Disciplinary Action: A single incidence of a serious or dangerous misbehavior, as well as chronic patterns of misbehavior, may result in the following:

- Parent Custody: Students are released to the parent for the remainder of the school day.
- Short-term Suspensions: The school principal may suspend a student for up to ten school days. The parent and student are immediately notified of the district's due process procedures.
- Long-term Suspensions: Suspensions of ten or more school days are subject to the approval of the superintendent. The student and parents are immediately notified of the district's due process procedure. In such suspensions, the student remains in school until appeal opportunities have been exhausted.
- Expulsions: The student and parents are informed when a student is subject to expulsion from school. Expulsion requires official action of the Governing Board. Formal notification includes instructions in the district's process procedures.

- Summary Suspensions: When the student's behavior causes a clear and present danger to self and/or others, a suspension may be immediate.

DUE PROCESS

In disciplinary cases, students are entitled to due process. Students must:

- be informed of the accusations against them
- have the opportunity to deny the accusations
- have explained to them the factual basis for the accusations
- have a chance to present an alternative factual position if the accusations are denied

VIOLATIONS OF THE LAW

Serious misbehavior is quite uncommon in our elementary schools. Violations of the law occasionally occur. We must report such offenses to the legal authorities. Some examples include:

- theft of school property
- destruction or defacement of school property
- arson
- assault and battery
- possession of weapons
- smoking tobacco products
- possession, use, or sale of alcohol and/or drugs

LIABILITY

Unfortunately, occasional vandalism at our schools has become a fact of life. People who damage school property may be held liable for these damages according to state law.

In the case of minor children, the parents are liable. District policy requires that parents be billed for the cost of the damage. We ask you to help us by teaching your child respect for public property.

APPENDIX
H

Student Behavior

EXPECTATIONS for student behavior and procedures for dealing with in-fractions of those behaviors are contained in the Student–Parent Hand-book. Please familiarize yourself with the procedure.

1. Care of Books and Equipment

   All textbooks and equipment available to student use are given a CFSD number. When books are checked out to students, the number of the book issued is recorded in the teacher's grade book next to the student's name.

   Teachers will be held responsible for inventory and care of the texts, workbooks, and equipment placed in their care. Each teacher is responsible for securing the return of all texts or payment for lost or damaged texts if necessary. If a student fails to return a book/work-book or make necessary payment for loss or damage, the teacher should notify the office so that a hold is placed on the student's records. Please note that this also applies to teachers' personal books or materials as long as an appropriate checkout system is main-tained.

2. Class Transition

   Procedures:
   a. Walk your students to all specialist classes when they move as a FULL class.
   b. Supervise your students in the hallways on their way to lunch.
   c. Supervise your students on their way to the bus.
   d. Emphasize with students (daily, if needed) their role in maintain-ing good self-discipline to and from classes when you cannot be with them (during backing, for instance).

e. All special area teachers need to be equally diligent in emphasizing good behavior prior to student's return to homeroom.

f. Specialists will walk with students to the buses at the end of the day if the students do not return to their homerooms.

3. Student Misbehavior

Canyon View School has set guidelines to ensure consistency in discipline on school premises. We want parents to know that school rules are designed to protect all children. Students who break the rules are treated firmly, kindly, and appropriately from day to day and from student to student.

Most students never have serious discipline problems. To protect the rights of all our children, it's important that parents and students understand the consequences of misbehavior. While each student is assessed individually, generally the following sequence will occur:

a. Option One:
   Class Behavior System: Each teacher will tell, explain, practice, and post class rules, consequences, and rewards.

b. Option Two:
   Informal Talk: The teacher will informally talk with the student to work out a plan of action to avoid the problem in the future.

c. Option Three:
   Quiet Room: School adults will follow the procedures established by the staff if students break school rules. See 4, Quiet Room Referral.

d. Option Four:
   Parent Conference: A conference with the teacher, principal, and parent may be held to formulate a behavior change plan.

e. Option Five:
   Privilege Suspension: The principal may notify the parent and student of privilege suspension. These privileges include bus, playground, MPR, computer lab, library, or participation in class or school.

4. Quiet Room Referrals/Procedures

a. Purposes:
   1) Provide students with opportunities to develop a plan of action to resolve conflicts and discipline problems in a supervised setting
   2) Provide a safe, caring, structured setting for students to cool off and reflect on their behavior

b. Procedures for Referral
   Quiet Room referral procedures are as follows:
   1) If a student breaks school rules:

- First: School adult tells/reminds the student what they are supposed to do. ("Please walk in the hallway.")
- Second: If the student doesn't comply right away with the school adult's request, a verbal warning will be issued. ("You now have a warning. I want you to. . . . If you choose to continue misbehaving, you'll be choosing to earn a Quiet Room referral.")
- Third: If student continues the misbehavior or does not comply right away, a referral is written; the student is told to report to the Quiet Room for the next lunch period. ("You now have a referral. I want you to . . . report to the Quiet Room tomorrow at _____ o'clock.")

2) If the student manifests one or more of the behaviors below:
- fighting
- blatant non-compliance
- blatant arguing
- endangering self or others

the following steps will be followed:
- First: Referral written, principal notified, parents notified.
- Second: Student spends at least three lunch periods in Quiet Room
  - Student *may* be escorted to the Quiet Room immediately (during lunch only).

c. Minor Offenses

1) If a child gets a referral for breaking school rules, he/she will:
- attend the Quiet Room the next lunch period
- formulate plans for future action
- agree to sign the plan, along with the Quiet Room aide and referring school adult

d. Major Offenses

1) If a child endangers himself/herself or others, blatantly argues or blatantly non-complies with school adult requests, the following will occur:
- A referral will be written.
- The Quiet Room aide will send a copy to the principal.
- Child attends Quiet Room for at least three lunch periods.
- Student, teacher, principal, parent, and Quiet Room aide sign the plan.
  - Student is responsible for taking the plan to adults for signatures.

e. Requirements

1) The student is to *automatically* report to the Quiet Room for the next lunch period after he/she receives a referral. Students must sign into the Quiet Room as they enter.

    2) If a child fails to show up for a referral, the Quiet Room aide will double the time to be served and notify the principal and the parent.

f. Quiet Room Rules

    1) Be on time.

    2) Raise hand before saying anything.

    3) Keep hands, feet, and objects to yourself.

    4) Follow teacher directions immediately.

    5) Write a plan you will follow.

    6) Work quietly.

g. Quiet Room Consequences

    1) 1st Break: Verbal warning

    2) 2nd Break: Additional time assigned

    3) 3rd Break: Principal notified, parents contacted

h. Pattern Behavior Problems

Individual behavior change plans for students manifesting patterns of misbehavior/inappropriate behavior will be cooperatively developed with principal, teacher, student, parent, and Quiet Room aide.

i. Student Procedures/Responsibilities

    1) Bring lunch.

    2) Eat for fifteen minutes.

    3) Sit at desk and remain quiet.

    4) Write a plan of action/change.

    5) Bring a plan to referring school adult who must agree to the plan and obtain appropriate signatures.

    6) Discuss plan with his/her parents.

j. Quiet Room Supervisor Responsibilities

    1) The aide is responsible for bringing pencils, scrap paper, and plan forms to the Quiet Room. The aide also reviews Quiet Room rules and procedures.

    2) The aide is responsible for reviewing steps a student needs to follow to develop good written behavior plan.

    3) The student is responsible for developing the initial plan on scrap paper.

    4) The student will raise his/her hand when ready to have their plan checked.

    5) The aide reviews the plan, asks questions, and helps clarify in the child's mind what is written.

    6) If the plan is not acceptable, the child will make modifications and then raise his/her hand.

    7) The aide reviews the plan and accepts or asks the child to again make modifications.

8) When the plan is acceptable, it is then written on a plan form by the student.

9) A final, acceptable copy of the written plan is brought to the aide and all appropriate parties sign.

10) Copies of the final plan go to the student, teacher, principal, and Quiet Room aide on the same day the plan is written.

11) Students remain in the Quiet Room for the remainder of the lunch break after the plan is written.

12) The Quiet Room aide should complete two checks on a child's plan in a two-week period.

13) The following day after students are released from the Quiet Room they will go to the area that the off-duty Quiet Room aide has been assigned for one day.

ALL COMPLETED BEHAVIOR PLANS SHOULD BE SENT TO THE PRINCIPAL WHEN THE CHECK DATES ARE COMPLETED.

QUIET ROOM FOLLOW-UP PROCEDURES

(1) The Quiet Room aide verbally and in writing notifies the outside aide, before the 10:15 recess, of those children who are to be supervised for the morning recess and lunch break.

(2) The outside aide tells the children where she will be on duty and tells them to check in with her when they arrive.

(3) The outside aide will specify the area where they can plan and suggest possible activities (i.e., read a book).

(4) If a child does not show up outside, the outside aide will check with the teacher and/or child for the reason he/she did not come. If the reason is legitimate, the child can go to the assigned area the next day. If the reason is not legitimate, the aide will complete a Quiet Room memo and assign the child to the Quiet Room for one day.

The Administrator Skills Inventory[2]

Directions

Please rate the administrator's skill in each of the areas listed below. Use the following rating scheme. Record your rating in the space to the left of each item.

Highly Competent	Competent	Average	Not so Competent	Incompetent
1	2	3	4	5

Rating

STUDENTS

_____ **1.** Planning and implementing effective and due process student discipline practices.

_____ **2.** Managing effective mainstreaming of disabled students.

_____ **3.** Developing and maintaining student leadership systems.

_____ **4.** Encouraging and maintaining positive student self-image.

_____ **5.** Other.

STAFF RELATIONS

_____ **6.** Organizing and conducting school site council responsibilities.

_____ **7.** Managing affirmative action practices and policies.

_____ **8.** Managing the district's contracts within Individual School Management System site council structures.

_____ **9.** Cooperatively planning budgets with staff and site council.

_____ **10.** Organizing accountability processes for administrative personnel.

[2]The Administrator Skills Inventory is reprinted with permission: Slezak, J. *Odyssey to Excellence.* San Francisco:Merritt (1984).

_____ **11.** Organizing and maintaining accountability for district office personnel.

_____ **12.** Managing personnel practices in marginally defined areas of contracts.

_____ **13.** Organizing and facilitating teacher staff development programs.

_____ **14.** Organizing and facilitating classified staff development programs.

_____ **15.** Defining staff performance standards.

_____ **16.** Refining shared decision-making processes.

_____ **17.** Defining administrator rights and responsibilities.

_____ **18.** Other.

COMMUNITY RELATIONS

_____ **19.** Creating and maintaining relations with parent club within site council structure.

_____ **20.** Organizing and facilitating community involvement in school programs.

_____ **21.** Using community resources in planning and programs.

_____ **22.** Developing and using effective communication systems with community and parents.

_____ **23.** Developing and using effective techniques in marketing.

_____ **24.** Other.

CURRICULUM AND PROGRAM DEVELOPMENT

_____ **25.** Planning and using needs assessment procedures.

_____ **26.** Profitably using program evaluation processes.

_____ **27.** Developing competency-based course requirements.

_____ **28.** Improving guidance and counseling practices.

_____ **29.** Developing and using learning centers.

_____ **30.** Developing and using effective instructional goals.

_____ **31.** Developing and using diagnostic procedures for classroom purposes.

_____ **32.** Other.

GENERAL MANAGEMENT

_____ **33.** Improving conflict resolution techniques.

_____ **34.** Improving plant and facilities management.

_____ **35.** Developing and managing differentiated staffing.

_____ **36.** Implementing data-based decision making.

_____ **37.** Organizing and using effective classified staff evaluations.

_____ **38.** Organizing and using effective certificated staff evaluations.

_____ **39.** Organizing and using effective administrative staff evaluations.

_____ **40.** Finding and using procedures for improving school climate.

_____ **41.** Finding and using procedures for improving personal well-being.

_____ **42.** Developing management by objectives processes.

_____ **43.** Improving time management procedures.

_____ **44.** Developing and using simulation games for improvement of management skills.

_____ **45.** Improving techniques for analyzing forces working for and against solutions to problems.

_____ **46.** Improving group process techniques.

_____ **47.** Other.

SUPERVISION AND EVALUATION

_____ **48.** Conducting teacher conferences.

_____ **49.** Selecting and organizing professional development in-service activities.

_____ **50.** Recognizing both good and not-so-good instructional practices and articulating the rationale for the decision.

_____ **51.** Dealing with teacher grievances.

_____ **52.** Articulating the theoretical foundations and the pros and cons for instructional and classroom management techniques.

Index